Mediterranean Sketches

Brewster Chamberlin

BY THE SAME AUTHOR

Kultur auf Trümmern. Berliner Berichte der
amerikanische Information Control Section, Juli bis
Dezember 1945 (1980)

A Piece of Paris: The Grand XIVth (1996)

Paris Now and Then.
Memoirs, Opinions and a Companion to the City of
Light for the Literate Traveler (2002)

MEDITERRANEAN SKETCHES

Fictions, Memories and Metafictions

by

Brewster Chamberlin

The Vineyard Press
Port Jefferson NY
2005

i

For Elizabeth and Ernest Koenig
With great affection

The Vineyard Press, Ltd.
106 Vineyard Place
Port Jefferson, NY 11777

Cover: oil painting by Fran Zak, *Mediterranean Views.*
Photos by Lynn-Marie Smith: Back cover, Shrine of Saint
Arsenius, Corfu, 2002. Author in the hills of Perithia,
Corfu, 2004.

No, it was neither I nor the world that counted, but solely the harmony and silence that gave birth to the love between us. A love I was not foolish enough to claim for myself alone, proudly aware that I shared it with a whole race born in the sun and sea, alive and spirited, smiling in complicity at the brilliance of its skies.

Albert Camus: "Nuptials at Tipasa"

I don't know, I think it's the sea urchins. Where else can you get such salty sea urchins. The Mediterranean gives them to you like an offering, thanking you for eating them. That's rare, you know.

Eden the Perfect Bartender at The
Edge Bar, Marseilles

Preface

These thus far fugitive pieces were written over a period of years for various purposes reflecting the time I've spent in the lands that border on and the islands that lie in the Mediterranean Sea. The larger Mediterranean world, basically Hellenic, Arab and Jewish in culture and world-views is the cement that holds these texts in a form of coherence. The formats of the sketches are eclectic reflecting their occasional nature, ranging from poetry through letters and short stories to what I have called "metafictions," meaning texts that are simultaneously true because based on personal experiences but also fiction because those experiences have been filtered through the requirements of the story being told or rearranged to evoke a mood or a thought, not necessarily to offer description.

It is in the nature of such compendia as this one that a certain amount of repetition is an ineluctable signature if the spontaneity of the occasion is to be retained. And since this spontaneity is in part what makes these things interesting to read, I hope readers do not find this to be too onerous. The pieces are meant to amuse and occasionally emotionally move the reader. Edification is a secondary but not unimportant consideration. One has whiled too long in the groves of academe to neglect The Pedagogic, but it should not egregiously intrude.

I owe a great debt of gratitude to my friend Richard Pine for his eagle eye in copy editing the text to save me from embarrassing misspellings and abuse of factual accuracy. Should any such infelicitous items remain, the fault is mine, not his. For their assistance in providing various sorts of information I am happy to thank Alexina and David Ashcroft and James Gifford. I am grateful to Robert DeMaria, The Vineyard Press' founder and director, for accepting the manuscript and seeing it through the press.

As always, this book is as much Lynn-Marie Smith's as it is mine.

Key West, January 2005

Table of Contents

III. Metafictions

I. FICTIONS

No Refuge for a Sinner

THE EXHAUSTED THIEF stumbled down the rue des Lices under the wall topped by a spiked iron fence that ran along the Coulège Sant Jóusè. Without thinking she swerved to the right onto the cobblestones of the rue des Teinturiers. Panting in short harsh gasps, she slowed her pace momentarily, searching with glazed desperate eyes down the narrow street. A thin canal separated the buildings on the right from the street proper, through which a desultory minor branch of the Sorgue River slowly flowed with too little force to turn the massive moss-covered waterwheels. Except for the chugging of the water and the rasping breath of the thief, silence lay lightly on the early morning air. The summer sun had risen a scant half hour earlier.

Up the left side of the street her eyes barely took in the small closed shops and restaurants with their brightly painted façades each of a different color. She would find no refuge there unless she broke into one of the stores and for that she had no time.

Her only chance of escape was to get off the street immediately and wait until the midmorning crowds filled the city's thoroughfares. In the mass of them she could move unnoticed until she reached the spotted yellow ramparts under which large omnibuses swallowed passengers bound for the towns and villages surrounding the old Pope's city of Avignon. She knew she could find a hiding place if she continued deeper into the twisting medieval lanes of the Quarter of the Cloth Dyers, but each passing second intensified her panic and brought her pursuers closer. She had no time for anything other than to remove herself from sight.

For a brief moment she rested against one of the waist-high cement plant containers that flank the small stone bridge across the canal leading to the dusty gray bulk of the Chapelle des Cordeliers rising stolidly out of the muddy water. Unsuccessfully trying to control her spasmodic breathing, she glanced up at the chapel and felt intimidated by the dark closed look of it; the tall narrow stained glass windows between the decaying flying buttresses seemed to soar into infinity above the rusting metal bellworks. Even the one sign of fallible humanity about it – a hole smashed into one of the windows – offered no comfort to her rattled brain. The faded green iron gate across the stone bridge blocked her way in any case. She pushed herself off the plant container not realizing the gate was open, but the chapel itself locked tight against the ravages of the infidel. All of this took no more than five seconds, during which she began to smell the slight odor of sewage that would increase in texture as the day's heat pressed into the canal.

Skirting a pile of blue and white plastic garbage bags, her left hand pressed against her side where a stitch began to yelp in pain, she continued erratically jogging along the low wall paralleling the canal against which she supported and propelled herself. Weaving through the row of plane trees shading the street as the sun rose higher in the blue eastern sky, the harried thief scuttled over the cobblestones like a manic crab at the bottom of a threatening lagoon, passing gray iron gates and a long iron fence guarding a deep green garden. She pushed briefly at the locked gate bars and hurried on, panic and exhaustion closing around her lungs and mind like a huge black vice. The brutal necessities of the situation screamed in a piercing whine through her stricken consciousness.

She tripped and fell on her hands and knees before another pair of dun colored wrought iron gates, which stood open on another short stone bridge over the canal. Behind the gates a scarred wooden door rested slightly ajar in the center of a gray pile of weather-gnawed rock. She crawled up the steps and scrambled through the gates, barely registering the sign that read: PENITENTS GRIS CHAPELLE SAINTE CROIX or the finely chiseled red letters carved over the entrance:

Venite Adoremus. Pushing the door inward only enough to allow her body to slip quickly inside, she closed it again exactly in the original position.

In the gloom of a long passageway she leaned against the wall to the left to calm her thundering heart and slow her grating breath spasms. Gradually her burning eyes focused on her silent surroundings and she saw in the dull half-light a closed blackened wooden door at the end of the corridor. She did not even consider the possibility that it would be locked. Slowly, then, the perception clarified: a church of some sort. If it were large enough and if they had not seen her enter and if they did not search it with care and if ... she would remain hidden for a few hours, then return to the street to be absorbed in the crowds and make her way to the buses. It was not Sunday so perhaps there would be no services. Her breathing slowed and relief began to loosen her stomach muscles.

Suddenly her intestines snapped painfully tight and she stopped breathing. Blood pounded through her head and rang deafeningly in her ears. The oppressive feeling that she was being watched gripped her chest and a strange force pulled her eyes up the wall against which she leaned. In a violent movement belying her exhaustion she jerked away from the wall, her arms shot up in an automatic gesture of self-protection, a shout of fear caught in her throat before it was expelled. She registered the agonized figure hanging on the bare whitewashed stone just below the arched wood-beamed ceiling. At first the nearly life-size crucified ivory body appeared to be covered with fresh blood and the thief shrank into herself, eyes widened in terror, legs trembling uncontrollably in the gloom. Slowly the stasis of insanity released its hold and her lungs began to move again. She squinted at the twisted form, no longer in terror, but with a deep misgiving of growing horror and distaste. The figure hung on the wall with dramatic effect, the yellowed white body lavishly splashed with red that appeared to spill from the long gash in the flesh of its right side and pour from the depths of the gored holes in its extremities. The theatrically realistic wounds and the ivory body of the blood splattered corpse elicited no sense of the miraculous, but rather something akin to disgust, though she could not tell whether her reaction or the blatant sensationalism of the figure caused it. Her throat dried, her tongue swelled and she swallowed only with effort. She could not remember what the letters INRI at the top of the cross signified and she felt a twinge of irritation.

Scrambling quickly down the chilly corridor away from the bleeding figure on the wall, the thief repressed a sudden desire to dash back through the door into the morning of the recognizable world. She hurried toward the far wooden door, past the only other object in the passageway: a large board on stilts onto which had been tacked pieces of paper in various shapes and colors announcing church related events and requesting contributions. The soft soles of her tennis shoes offered no sound to the possibility of echoes in the passage. Cautiously, she pushed the heavy door forward, then quickly slipped inside and gently closed it. A dull beam of light from a small window near the cupola vaguely illuminated the small empty antechamber of cold stone. A niche the width of a human arm in one wall housed the only decoration in the room: a virgin and child icon, each figure with a metal crown of appropriate size on its head.

The thief's apprehension increased as the cold of the building chilled the sweat on her forehead and back. She forced herself to breathe in slow, regular hisses of air through her nostrils and she rubbed the back of her legs to calm the spasms that rippled through the thigh muscles. She thought she heard voices somewhere – perhaps at the street door. An unexpected sneeze doubled her body at the waist, resounding in the narrow room. Bent in half, she froze in panic waiting for some reaction. From this contorted position, pinned in the eternity of a second, she stared at the third wooden door, not seeing the two small hand-lettered signs requesting visitors not to smoke and to respect the holy purpose for which the building had been erected. Her mind registered only the fact of the door, concentrating on that single aspect, knowing only that she must open it and find a place to hide, a refuge in which to rest and regain her balance, to quell her growing sense of foreboding and fear. Her body shook as she straightened and she wondered if the church had another exit. Of course. It must have: fire regulations. Her scattered thoughts did not coalesce around the absurdity of this conclusion: with a short sigh of relief she stepped to the door and pushed it open.

The thin squeak pierced her numbed brain with the force of a lightning bolt. She thought her heart would burst in her chest as bright lights exploded behind her eyes and she fell to the floor, losing consciousness for several seconds. Her fingers felt the thin cloth runner and the wood flooring worn down by thousands of pilgrim feet. The aged and battered wood had groaned as she stepped on it. She lay in the doorway of the large square room, its funeral darkness brightened only by a few guttering votive candles and light straining through one of the two stained glass windows high up the walls. Rows of chairs facing the right toward the arched entrance to the chapel proper stood in silent, accusing communion. The archway, framed in filigreed ironwork with the date 1818 at its apex, led to a long narrow chapel that ended at a gold painted altar glowing eerily in the darkness from an unseen source of light. In the upper reaches of the building wind moaned through the crevices of the tower, keening softly in the dimness of the chapel.

She dragged herself up off the floor, holding onto the back of a prayer stool, and staggered to the chapel entrance. Down the aisle the pews remained invisible in the murk, the stained glass windows here, three on each side, and four candles burning on the altar only emphasized the lack of light and she did not see the large grimed paintings of religious themes hanging from the walls above the wood wainscoting down the length of the room. In fact, she saw nothing except the strangely illuminated altar with its background: an abstract representation of a cross as a sunburst enclosed in a larger blooming sunburst of painted gold in which the heads and wings of angels floated peacefully. The center of the smaller sunburst appeared to move in slow pulsations to an unrecognizable rhythm, hanging in the air at the end of the dark hall, expanding and contracting in an ancient tempo that began to pull her toward it. The purest form of fear countered the magnetism of the undulating glow as the shapes of the half-seen icons in the cold gray chiaroscuro pressed down on her. Shadows beckoned and in the briefest of moments she saw in the center of the sunburst her own soul in blood-soaked agony burning away in the gold bright expansion of light.

With a wrenching cry she tore herself away from the sight and blindly rushed backward into one of the wardrobe-like cubicles used for confession. Panic ripped away the edges of her mind and raced toward the core of her sanity as she plunged out of the battered confessional and blundered into a small stone chapel directly across the room from the doorway through which she had come. This bare gray room glowed with a softer greenish emanation filtered through the diamond-patterned stained glass in a door through which she threw herself. Her rapid fumbling at the iron handle rattled the door, but she could neither force it nor concentrate her diminished energy to break through the glass. The shadows moved closer about her, darkening even the greenish light from the garden door, and with a massive wail of horror bursting from her chest, the thief unseeing and no longer able to think ran back through the series of doors, not heeding the noise she made in her dash for the safety of the street.

She did not look at the crucified figure on the wall as she threw open the final door and rushed past the first of the beggars to gather at the entrance. In the bright sunlight of the morning she stopped by the iron gates to the chapel. Relief lifted her up out of herself and her face gradually relaxed into a blank smile. With increasingly sure movements she walked into the rue des Teinturiers to find the protection of the authorities.

Settling himself in his usual position, the beggar shook his head at the retreating figure, happy at not having to share the take with anyone else at the early morning mass.

(Avignon, 1983)

The Professional

THEY CAME OVER THE RIDGE one by one wearing
leather jackets, their guns held loosely in the
crooks of their arms. Looking through the glasses
he saw they were very sure of themselves and were
laughing at the jokes they tossed back and forth.
They were speaking in Provençal, which he did not
understand, but understanding was no longer
necessary. The hunters had been up long before
dawn as soon as the woman in the village had
given the alarm. He knew now for certain she had
not died soon enough. She was not supposed to
have been there at all, only her husband, the object
of his mission. That much had been accomplished,
but the woman had come in so unexpectedly that
his aim had been off. The panic that followed had
been very unprofessional. But then, becoming
involved in a blood vendetta had not been very
professional either. Perhaps he'd been in the
business too long.

The panic had made it possible for them to
follow his trail through the hills above the village

and he cursed for once the lack of the mistral. The sun began to hurt his eyes and he lowered the glasses with a sigh. He checked the pistol and rolled over to wait for them. He had never been this close to it before, it had never been so inevitable before, and he wondered how he would die in the end. He would find out soon enough, but then it would be too late.

(Tavel, 1983)

The Last Summer Together

SOMETIMES WE WENT TO THE MOVIES in the afternoon to get away from the heat. The year before, the owner of the theater had installed an air-conditioning unit with lavish ceremony. It was the only air-conditioned building in the small seashore town. The owner's cousin in Chicago had written to him that the investment would increase attendance, as of course it did, considerably. We went to get out of the heat, not to see the films, but we all paid the same price.

The air-conditioning machine made so much noise you couldn't hear the soundtrack very well. This did not make any difference to us because all the movies were dubbed in Greek and we had not mastered the language beyond the phrases necessary to make our basic wishes known and understood. This annoyed our parents who believed children learned foreign languages faster than adults. What we learned quickly enough was to get what we asked for in the stores and at the drink stands on the beach. Since we spent most of our time alone together this level of knowledge satisfied us.

We went to the movies because it was cooler there than in the town or on the beach. We sat comfortably through some pretty bad movies to be out of the sun and heat for a few hours. That was at the height of the summer, the year we spent the vacation on the Greek island. Our father was working up a new project and our mother was browning herself and laughing a lot. Mostly we didn't have much to do with them. Mostly we were out together with our own games. Our parents remained on the edges of the summer that year, gray and indistinct in the pale orange of the island sunshine, despite mother's earnest and successful attempt to deepen the color of her skin.

One reason we didn't learn more of the language that year was the fact that we played by ourselves and had little to do with the local children. Most of the kids our ages on vacation came from the north and spoke languages we already knew something about, however ungrammatically. The local children usually had to work. They were not on vacation. I thought then they couldn't have vacations until they were much older and earned more than their parents who never took vacations. So we rarely had to do with the Greek children and most of the others we didn't like and so ignored them whenever we could.

In any case, we had enough to interest us and we did not miss the company of others. That summer, the last one we spent together as children, the three of us were self-contained in our own private world of sun and new pleasures. If the adults we met thought us obnoxious, we made no attempt to deliberately be so. We simply found no use for them and acted accordingly. We did not behave badly and usually followed the dictates of our parents who absently told us to go to bed long after the usual hour. We were indifferent to their concerns as they, for the most part, were to ours. We had other interests that summer. Knowledge did not spoil our pleasures. Our mental baggage was of a more innocent nature and we suffered no emotional histories. It was not until the end of the summer, after we had exhausted the possibilities of the small island, that I at least began to notice things that would eventually change me profoundly and make me, later on, an adult, no matter how hard I resisted.

But, as I say, the summer began in the innocence of those who have never smoked, drank or experienced sex as adults know it. We arrived to take possession of the rented house two streets away from the beach, and we prowled the neighborhood to orient ourselves while our parents crawled the pubs and slept late in the mornings. We had always enjoyed a large amount of freedom, a result of our parents' concern with assuring a liberated development of their children, and this increased during vacations when standards relaxed a little. So we were left to our own inventions for most of the day.

Once we had scouted out the lay of the land, as it were, we fell into a series of patterns that changed so often they did not become routine. We did not set out to learn anything beyond the geography, vegetation and the possibilities of enjoyment on that part of the island we could call our own. But in the nature of things, of course, we learned much more, more than we wanted to know or knew how to digest.

When we walked unsteadily off the ferry onto the stained wood dock the first day, our skin was the slightly sickish color of northern winter and our hair was various shades of northern light brown. As the summer progressed we children browned our flesh and haphazardly bleached our hair to golden white as we played in the sun. Our parents' skin browned also, but they worked hard to achieve the effect that came to us naturally. After the first couple of days we safely ignored adult suggestions regarding the use of suntan oils and our skin never blistered or hurt with splotches of red and pink pain.

First, we looked into the immediate area around the house. The war had been over for less than ten years and the great tourist boom had not yet blighted the landscape, our neighbors did not intrude their noises and intimacies upon us. There remained a large amount of open space that we filled with our cries of discovery and pleasure. A small grove of lemon trees grew in our backyard and we tasted the bitter fruit daily until the woman who came to clean indicated that the lemons would not ripen for another month, a bit of knowledge we greeted with indifference. Our father used the lemons in a drink called "gin sour." The lemons alone were sour enough for us. Sam, my youngest brother who had not reached his sixth birthday, developed a taste for green lemons and persisted in this affectation even though Ingemar, called Inky, and I, Adela, called Della, laughed at his precocity. We informed him with grave seriousness that his skin would turn green, but we ruined the effect by bursting into laughter when his face clouded with doubt. After that it was difficult to make him believe anything we told him.

Behind the house, the mountains rose up brown and green as if to protect us from whatever lay on the other side. We never felt particularly in need of that protection, but it was comforting to see the massive promontories in the distance, always there when we woke in the morning. No matter what happened down on the shore, we thought, the mountains would always be there. One day we rode up into them on rented donkeys with a wicker picnic basket and that was pleasant enough, although we children preferred to have them at a distance, mysterious and somehow offering us safety.

Father thought the fishing would be good in the mountain streams and mother said you could swim in the pools without bathing suits. This was before the time of topless and nude beaches unless you belonged to a *naturaliste* organization. Neither of those subjects interested us very much. Nudity was not uncommon in our house and fish were fine to eat, but we couldn't imagine having to catch them.

The beach and the odd corners and squares of the town interested us more than anything else. We could all swim after a fashion and I, at least, became quite good at it as the summer wore on. We played games in the water and built structures with the wet sand of the beach that disappeared during the night and sometimes during the day if the wind came up to lift the water.

When the sand and sea bored us, we would move through the dusty streets of the town, always careful to reappear at our rented house on time for meals to avoid the punishment of being kept indoors. I've never been sure how we did this since we had no watches; perhaps we checked with the clock on the town hall tower in the main square from time to time.

The narrowest back lanes of the older section of the town interested us most of all. In spite of our lighter color we walked without undue interest shown us amidst the locals: children, if they are relatively quiet, can be invisible and we practiced invisibility with care. We saw a great deal that way, some of which we did not understand.

18

We began looking into windows and the open doors of the houses and buildings along the back streets where people lived away from the shops of the harbor and the tourists. In the afternoons it was like looking at pictures in a museum. Food and the heat made people lethargic and they moved slowly if at all at midday. Everyone rested in the afternoon except the tourists on the beach who could afford the time. When we weren't at the movies to get away from the heat, we toured the windows, which was much more fun.

Gradually each of us chose a few favorite windows behind which certain static scenes appeared, repeated with only minor variations each time we peered into the rooms.

Some windows presented more problems than others. This occurred when people closed the shutters or curtains to keep out the heat and prying eyes. Since we respected their desire for privacy we never spent too long attempting to see through the cracks in the wooden shutters and rips in the curtains. Standing too long before a door or window would have called attention to us. Besides, there were enough open windows and doors to satisfy our curiosities.

Sam liked open doors the best because he couldn't see into most of the windows unless Inky or I held him up. We did this reluctantly, since he weighed a lot for his age and too often wanted to know why we found such and such a scene interesting. He liked scenes with animals best. He understood animals, I guess. He was also very good about being quiet on our rounds. He even learned to do a passable imitation of us rocking with silent laughter or giggling with no more noise than a feather falling in the air.

For some reason, Inky liked the sleepers and could stare for minutes on end at figures napping. Something about the openness of their faces in sleep and the rumbling of their stomachs as they digested lunch appealed to his sense of humor. He especially enjoyed the occasions when the sleepers farted and mumbled an automatic apology without waking. When this happened Inky's face turned purple with suppressed laughter and we had to quickly move on. As summer slowly wound its way into August, Inky began to collect snores during the afternoons and at one point he identified twenty-eight varieties, many of which he practiced aloud to our parents' dismay and delight.

For myself, I didn't really have a favorite scene to collect, although both Sam and Inky insisted I did and was keeping it a secret. If this had been true the secret was very well kept, even from me. I suppose I had reached the age in which I found it difficult to identify completely with anything, a time in my life when I was no longer a little girl, but not yet a pubescent female. It was a limbo period about which I remained happily unconscious that summer, at least until our vacation neared its end.

In any case, I did like the quieter scenes with little movement and no yelling: an old woman seated in a rocking chair sewing or a fisherman at the kitchen table repairing a piece of equipment. If these scenes contained no animals or sleeping figures my brothers became restless and we had to move on, so I rarely had the opportunity to really study them. Under the circumstances, I didn't mind and let myself be guided by the small enthusiasms that drew the others from house to house, enjoying the relative invisibility and the lack of necessity to think about anything for very long.

We floated like this on the surface of the days, observing the varieties of life without intruding ourselves into the scenery before us. Being strangers on the island made it easier for us because the scenery did not intrude itself into our lives very deeply. The reality of the lives we observed remained distant or unintelligible to us until one afternoon in August when we made an excursion into a new street, closer to the harbor than we usually went.

Sam saw nothing in the room because the window was too high and I dragged them away before he could demand to be lifted up. Inky didn't recognize either the scene or the people because I pushed them both down the street before anything could register on his mind. At least he never acted as if he had really seen anything and I never explained it or even talked with him about it.

Fortunately for them I reacted fast enough. But I saw it, and recognized one of the people in the room. That image has remained with me ever since, only slightly fuzzy from use and the corrosive effect of passing years. So much skin shining with effort, facial expressions distorted with what seemed to be unbearable pain made incomprehensible to me by the sounds of muted joy in their throats as they moved in a jerking rhythm unknown to me then.

It could not have lasted more than a few seconds, my view of the scene, then my instinctive reaction shoved us away from the window and down the street toward the beach.

It never mattered who the man was, but our mother's expression of abandon remained with me long after the same expression distorted my own features. In later years understanding did not bring forgiveness with it and I learned the art of repression early.

Outwardly nothing changed during the rest of the vacation on the island. The sun continued its daily march across the sky with the inevitability of time; the sea continued to give us meals and refresh our heated bodies. In fact, nothing changed at all even afterward, as we continued to grow up in an apparently satisfactory manner. Not outwardly, not for the others perhaps. But to this day I avert my eyes from windows I pass in the street and avoid going to movies whenever possible.

(Avignon, 1992)

Achmed's Universe-Shattering Volume
or
The Great Horn of Alexandria
(A Fable)

(For Richard Hood)

ONE LONG, BEIGE SUMMER DAY, as the dust-laden heat crushes mere mortals with its midday weight, Achmed the Young Mechanic feverishly labors on in the confines of his ochre-brown, oil-soaked matchbox workshop deep in the Bab Sidra quarter of the city, Alexandria, fabled capital of Alexander's empire, site of the great Library and the giant Pharos Lighthouse, formerly a cosmopolitan urban center of European and Arab culture, now an Egyptian city, the second city of the Egyptian Arab Republic, poorer in its multicultural milieux, with no redeeming European features, but no filthier than before.

Here amidst the oil-bespattered dust globs, sweating fiercely, pale young Achmed in his tiny shop on an obscure narrow side street builds with tense patience the implement that will bring him fame and renown in the Middle East and beyond, a veritable mechanism that will burst his name onto the very consciousness of the world: none will ever forget his deed.

Because throughout the lands of this sorely tried and war-torn region of abysmal poverty and abominable ignorance, straining against a narrow tranche of wealth and university education, there is but one thing that transcends national, ethnic, and religious differences: the motor vehicle horn. It makes no matter whether the horn is fitted into a motorcar, a small or large truck, a van, an omnibus. No, it is not the type or size of motor vehicle that matters, it is the size and volume capacity of the horn itself. Whilst in other cultures and parts of the world, men have found other methods to express their masculinity, their power, and their authority over their environments and each other, here in the great historical soup-mix of Muslim, Jew and Christian, men have chosen the motor vehicle and its horn as the symbol and practical expression of their gender's traditional role of dominance.

Where else in the world can one find the precision and grace, the smoothness of transition, with which the Egyptian driver attempts to terrorize his fellow-drivers on the sizzling hot macadam of roads urban and rural, and achieves the perfect terrorization of his passengers as he weaves, slippery as a copper eel, in and out of the traffic lanes. Whether the lanes point in his or in the opposite direction is irrelevant to the necessary expression of his courage, and his indifference to invoices to repair bent and scraped fenders and doors. Of what value can a few scratches and deformations to the motor vehicle's body be, after all, compared to the pungent satisfaction of wreaking red havoc upon the mental and emotional equilibrium of tourist and native alike.

And all this perfection of hand to eye coordination is perfectly implemented at breathless speeds rarely even attempted in other regions of the civilized urban world.

And the Egyptian motor vehicle driver, most particularly the Alexandrian driver, conducts this quotidian mechanical ballet of the thoroughfares, such as the 26 of July Avenue along the Grande Corniche, Saad Zaghloul Street, and El Horreya Avenue, amidst a baffling, piercing, roaring cacophony rarely heard in other regions of the civilized world, despite the ubiquity of that scourge of modern human history, the internal combustion engine gasoline-powered motor car. For here drivers give pride of place to the motor vehicle horn in the same manner as drivers in other parts of the civilized world depend upon their motor vehicles' brakes to ensure their safety of arrival at their chosen destinations. Here, too, the horn's sound, shriller than a shofar, blatantly warns everyone on the street that the driver approaches.

And it is here, at this veritable nub of Egyptian male propriety, that Achmed plans to make his name, so to speak.

For what Achmed has created, and will soon install in his ancient green Lada 1200, is a complex, elaborate system of many-colored wires, electric current conductors, and sound boxes, which has turned his battered former taxi cab into an incredible loudspeaker to explode the single sound of a horn so powerful, of such a cosmically shattering volume, that it can be used only once, for it will deafen the entire city and bring all Alexandria's activities to a standstill – all human activity will instantly petrify at this sound, blasted into stone at the level of a nuclear explosion, hitherto only dreamed of by paranoid physicists and national security experts, regardless of nationality.

The Young Mechanic now with trembling hands addresses himself to the brief, but painfully composed and written message he will nail to the dusty, sun-yellowed wooden door of his dusty, black-oil smeared repair shop. Thereafter, he will walk with pulse pounding in his ears and heart rhythmically gasping for oxygen to the public baths on Masgued Sultan Street, where, in the privacy of a small dank and decay-smelling wooden cabin, he will conduct upon himself the age-old rites of purification by water.

When he completes this preliminary step, he will start the green Lada's engine, finger the soothing smoothness of his chain of pastel worry beads to calm his jumping nerve ends, and he will drive off to the corner of El Nabi Daniel and Mohafza Streets, brown eyes glittering brightly with the anticipation of the holy seer, a mild wan smile of expected transcendence hovering about his lips, will drive off to conduct his great Egyptian act, perfectly secure in the knowledge that, thereafter, his name would achieve the unforgotten historical heights and ancient splendor of the Pharaohs, the great Alexander himself, the Beatles....

And the world would never be the same again.

(Alexandria, Egypt - Washington DC, August 1996)

The Salvation Market

THE TOWN OF APT IS VERY COLD IN THE WINTER
AND CAN BE unbearable when the mistral slashes
through the Calavon Valley, exploding the icy air
into every crack in the buildings. The inhabitants
of the town on the edge of the Luberon mountain
range have an old tolerance that allows survival
and a measure of sanity. But foreigners do not feel
comfortable in Apt in the winter.

The two of them had enjoyed the deceptively
mild autumn and they thought they would wait out
the winter to enjoy the spring in Provence in their
rented house on the side of the hill overlooking the
valley. It was such a pretty view of the vineyards
and the olive trees and they were learning the
language at a satisfactory rate. They really did not
have much to do except drive their secondhand
automobile around the countryside to visit the old
castles and quaint villages. The Saturday morning
market of Apt was a special pleasure for them.

They loved the stalls and strange cheeses of
goat milk and odd-tasting sausages hung above the
counters of the trucks that became stores when
their sides were let down. They enjoyed sitting in
the café window across the crowded square from
the Mairie watching the bustle of the market and

listening to the dialects being spoken. They did not understand the words, but they liked the sounds. They bought sweaters against the cold and pistachio nuts to eat as they walked slowly up and down the narrow streets looking at the items offered for sale. They thought it would be interesting to try the horsemeat, but they never bought any.

As the winter closed in on them the market became the one thing they could look forward to each week. It soon became apparent that the winter was decreasing the size of the market and eventually even the heartiest of the farmers and businessmen gave up coming until the spring. When this happened they had little to look forward to each week. Gradually they began to spend more and more time alone trying to keep the house warm and going into town only briefly to buy food.

Then not only the freezing mistral raged through the valley, but unexpected and explosive emotions howled about the isolated stone house on the hillside with the pretty view. Then they no longer went to town at all. Soon smoke no longer blew from the chimney and wild dogs began to scratch at the locked door. Letters from their friends went unanswered until consulate officials returned them at the end of the winter.

(1984)

A Change of Life

(For Edith Fidler)

ONCE HE DISCOVERED he could no longer paint from real life, human or otherwise, the old painter remained for most of each day in his villa on the hillside above the sea. The southern wall of his studio contained enough window space so that the Mediterranean sun filled the large room and he only needed electricity at night or during a storm. When his wife questioned him on the subject, he said he could no longer see the objects of his attention and would have to imagine them in the studio. His wife accepted this without hesitation as the truth and adjusted the rituals of her days so she would not disturb his work.

The painter's friends, whom he allowed to visit him after his fame made it impossible for him to travel freely, first noticed the change when he received them in the massive kitchen he had constructed to indulge his occasional pleasure in preparing meals. He no longer invited them to see his latest vision of the Provence landscape or the brightly colored representations of the local villagers. They noticed a certain distraction in his attention and the fact that he drank mostly mineral water instead of his usual bottle of Tavel rosé.

They remarked that his hands absent-mindedly cupped his genitals and that he seemed to concentrate only when making something to eat. He continued to feed them wonderfully pungent meals made with ingredients that his wife purchased at the village market. After they left, they decided their old friend was in the process of working out some difficult technical problem and would return to normal after he solved it. Most of them were painters and writers so they could appreciate this state of affairs.

His dealer in the capital and the sympathetic critics, who had followed his long career from the early years of poverty and obscurity, viewed the change with concern and wondered what it could mean for his work. They wondered for a long time because he stopped sending canvases and drawings to Paris. When they called on him he showed his usual distant politeness, but evaded any questions about his recent work. Their admiration for the old man, and their dependence upon his production, was so great that they did not press the issue and they went away dissatisfied and troubled.

For a time he continued to order the usual amount of paints and canvas from the shop in one of the larger towns on the coast, but his wine merchant received a telephone call from the old man's wife, severely reducing the number of bottles sent to the villa every two weeks.

Through his wife and secretary, who came three times a week to help with the correspondence, he refused all invitations and informed his dealer he would not have an exhibition of new works the following year as had been planned. He would, however, continue to consider illustrating volumes of poetry and fiction with drawings. When the dealer, a friend and associate of many decades, called to discuss the matter, the old man refused to speak with him. He was too busy, his wife said politely.

As time went on the merchants who did business with the famous painter's villa on the lush verdant hillside above the sea noticed further changes in items they packed and sent off by truck. Orders to the paint store for colors and canvas ceased entirely, though drawing paper and crayons continued to be required and delivered. The wine-seller began taking orders for port and sherry wines and certain expensive reds and whites from northern vineyards. This surprised him because the painter had for years served nothing but the local wines. The village merchants remarked on the changes in purchases made by the painter's wife and the femme de ménage of the villa. Previously, the meals prepared in the painter's kitchen had been made with the simple, fresh products of the region. Now the shopping lists contained more esoteric and elaborate ingredients. On a visit to the large town on the coast, the painter's wife opened an account with a store that supplied unusual and hard to find kitchen utensils.

The painter began to spend less time in the crowded studio and more in the kitchen, from which he banned members of the household during the periods he spent there. Once again his friends noticed the difference first, as the meals they ate at his table became increasingly elaborate in construction and taste, so different from the spare simplicity of previous meals in the villa. The painter himself changed also. No longer did his friends find him abstractedly scratching his groin or missing large parts of the conversation. The concentration for which he was known returned. He rarely talked about painting, however, although he followed his friends' discussions with polite interest. He did talk at great length about food and cooking.

When one of his friends finally asked him about the changes and what they meant, the painter smiled and with great seriousness replied, "I am reinventing the nation's cuisine. Isn't that a marvelous thing to be doing?"

Boats of Passage

THE WATER LAPPED AT THE PEBBLES, making small coronas of foam that quickly disappeared as the tide formed new ones. The man sitting on the beach desultorily poked a stick at the foam coronas as they formed and disappeared. He looked out to the sea where dark boats moved from left to right across the horizon, carrying people from Sête to Oran to work on the fortifications.

Tired of digging holes in the pebbles, the child said, "When is mummy coming back?"

The man turned his sad eyes away from the boats carrying the people and jabbed the stick into the small lines of foam between his feet. "She won't be back until she gets better," he said.

"When will she get better?"

"The hospital is a good place for her now. She'll get better there."

"But when will she come back here?"

"We'll be going soon, love, she'll come to where we are when she's better."

"I don't want to go anywhere. Mummy will come here when she gets out of the hospital," the child insisted.

"We have to go," the man said. "Our lease is up and we have a new place in Madrid. You'll like Madrid. Mummy will meet us there."

"How will she know where we are?"

"The doctors and nurses will tell her, love. Don't worry about it now."

"Why can't I see her in the hospital?"

"Remember, I told you. She wants to be better again when she sees you. She doesn't want you to see her sick. She loves you." The man looked out at the boats moving very slowly across the horizon.

"What if they forget?"

"I've told them exactly where we'll be. They'll tell her that."

The child turned in a circle several times then stood still watching the boats out to sea. "Are we going home after mummy comes back? I want to go home," the child said in a small clear voice.

"Yes," the man said in a soft tone and looked at the boats. "Don't we all." Then he said in a louder, firmer voice, "But we can't right now. You know that, love, we've talked about it, haven't we? There are people who want to hurt your mummy and me. We have to stay away for a while."

"Why can't I go to school here?"

"You don't speak the language, love, you wouldn't understand the teacher."

"I didn't understand the teacher at home."

"I know, but that's different."

"Why can't we wait for mummy here, at the beach?"

"Our lease is up, love, we've got to move out."

The child fell silent and they both watched the boats. "Mummy will meet us when she's better."

"Yes, love, just as soon as she's better she'll come back to us."

"They'll tell her, the nurses, where we are."

"That's the first thing they'll tell her when she gets better. They promised."

"Maybe she'll get better tomorrow before we leave."

"I don't think so, love, but she'll meet us in Madrid."

They both looked at the boats for a minute.

"Mummy will know where we are in Madrid," the child said.

The man poked at the foam with the stick. "Absolutely," he said. "Absolutely, love."

(October 1997)

A Truly Simple Story

WHILE SIPPING AN APERITIF on the warm veranda of the Royal Hotel facing the Liston in Corfu Town, Colonel (Ret.) Ghastly studiously ignored the loud conversation being conducted as a monologue by the large florid American woman to her rather fuzzy diminutive female companion at the next table. The Colonel had had occasion in the recent past to swell with frustration at the inability of the heavy Madame Stone to converse about anything other than herself for more than a whisper of minutes. He had also felt the sharp tines of Mrs. Tooklah's dagger-like responses to some of his more outlandish opinions, which he insisted on expressing in the dry monotone of his native Bostonian speech.

Unfortunately for the Colonel's peace of mind, the two women appeared to possess a taste in holiday locales all too similar to his own. They encountered each other far too frequently, and these days the Colonel reached for the pen to sign in at the hotel front desks with trepidation and a brief flutter of mild anxiety. He was at this point bound to hear that piercing American voice bawling a great "HELLO THERE, GENERAL!" or suffer the galleon-like figure sailing with her smaller tugboat in tow across his line of vision, no matter where he perched for a week or two. He knew of course a perfect solution to the problem that did not require him to murder the creature: he could return to the United States where, he was certain, he would never hear or see them again. The only flaw in this resolution to the matter was the fact that the Colonel could not himself return to the country of his birth without running too great a risk.

So now they all sat within meters of each other in the diminishing heat of the Ionian summer evening and he could for the life of him not shut out the raucous tones of Mme Stone's authoritative statements on the value of American popular songs in representing American culture to the rest of the world. Why, he wondered, was this necessary in the olive and retsina-laden air of Corfu, when there was so much Greek culture, popular as well, to be appreciated?

"The only songs are simple songs and we Americans write the simplest and thus the truest songs. It is all very clear and straight-forward," the sunburned expert pronounced.

"Rather simple, in fact?" the Colonel ventured. If he could not have peace, he would join the war.

"Exactly. Simple and true," Mrs. Tooklah confirmed with the weight of finality in her voice.

"The Trail of the Lonesome Pine," Mme Stone ended that conversational topic and, to the

Colonel's dismay, moved immediately on to the next.

(Corfu, 2000)

Dead Waters

WHY DID HE CHOOSE THIS GODFORSAKEN PLACE?
Because it's what it is.
He certainly didn't pick it because of what Henry James wrote about it.
The sunsets are prodigious, or so Barrès said. But that was long ago.
Who's he?
A Frenchman
Well, there you are.
I am not precisely sure why he chose this town, and this hotel. Nostalgia perhaps.
Gives him the feeling of being close to the folk, no doubt.
No, I don't think he considered that.
Aigues-Mortes. What does it mean?
Dead waters, I believe. One of the Crusades left from here.
He's never been interested in that subject.
Nor is he now. Perhaps he thinks it's a good place to die. Perhaps he likes the idea of being surrounded by walls. The isolation. Who knows? The sea …
But we're miles from the sea.
It wasn't always that way, you see.

41

Very funny.

Mildly amusing, perhaps.

Anything new?

No. The physician reports no change.

Is he writing?

Not for three weeks that I know of.

He's always so damned secretive. My other authors show me everything as soon as they get words on paper. I never see anything of his until he thinks it's ready for the printer. Why did he ask us to come here anyway? We've not seen him for more than a few minutes.

If we hadn't already been in Europe he wouldn't have asked. Perhaps he's afraid of being alone.

It's like being at a wake before the corpse is a corpse. I can't say I feel comfortable. Something about necrophilia ...

Imagine what he must feel ... such a gift being snuffed out before he's thirty.

I must say I can't imagine him feeling much of anything ... except for his work. There's emotion enough in that. That's where it all goes. I've been his publisher for eight years and I've rarely seen him show any feeling at all.

It's his work that's important, the only thing in the end.

This horrible wind is enough to drive a person mad. Does it ever end?

They say it blows in units of three days: three or six or nine, but sometimes not. One of the mysteries of the region. Makes the heat bearable.

Place will be overrun with tourists in a few years. They're already swarming along the Côte d'Azur.

Famous artists and the sun. Soon the artists leave and the tourists remain in the sun. It's an old story.

Don't mean to sound heartless, but I hope something happens soon. I've got to get back to New York.

He'll die soon enough. He wants you to take the last manuscript back with you. That's all he does now, the corrections.

And when he's finished then he'll be ready to die …

Something like that, I suppose.

In that case, I'd correct forever.

But he won't.

What about the woman and the child? Christ, that's all we need. There's always a woman and a child, isn't there? To complicate things?

He made some provisions for them. There isn't much left, but they won't starve.

He made a fair amount of money in the last few years. I know, I sign the royalty checks.

I don't think he's ever been too cautious with money.

Can't have much left if this place is any indication. What a shabby hotel.

It's very old and he stayed here years ago. Shall we go out for a stroll and a pastis? It is rather close in here.

Walk in this wind? No thanks. I should say not. Is that the yellow lickerish stuff?

Yes. Or an absinthe? I think one can still get that here, if one asks in the right way. What do you say?

Do they have any scotch, do you think? They must have at least one bottle of scotch in this dump.

We can ask the innkeeper.

It's the heat, this endless heat that gets you down.

If he can stand it, I think we can too. It won't be long now.

It doesn't make any difference to him, he's dying.

Here's the innkeeper now.

Well, monsieur, you are correct about one thing: not even the painters come here now. No picturesque local costumes. And the heat, the mosquitoes are vicious. In the winter the mistral blows all the time. Spring is nice. But very few tourists come here. They go to the Saintes-Maries or to the Côte d'Azur where they can be taken care of. Hardly anyone comes to Aigues-Mortes, except an occasional traveler, if you know the difference.   Perhaps the name frightens them. Some times we have those who come to die, like your friend, if you don't mind my saying so. It's like that here, you see.   Appropriate perhaps. Would you care for a drink? We do have some old scotch and you will not have long to wait.

The Rub

THEY LIKED LIVING IN THE SOUTH in a small village near the golden walled city of the popes, fabled city where Petrarch first and finally saw Laura, Avignon. It was no longer the city of Petrarch or the popes, of course, the twentieth century saw to that. This was why they so much liked living in the village; it hadn't changed much in its architecture and its streets still wound narrow through the heat of the summer, ignoring the automobiles and mopeds that buzzed through them.

They liked the privacy of living behind a high stone wall cut by an iron gate large enough to drive their small car through. The far end of the garden overlooked the valley leading to the highway, the garden of fig and olive trees and colorful flowers sheltered them from the brilliant sunlight of midday when they ate lunch in the shade.

They liked the feeling of wearing only a pair of shorts and sleeveless tops in the summer heat that allowed them to enjoy spontaneous love-making during the day. They liked the variety of loving in different positions in the different rooms in the house. He was particularly fond of the deep valley between her full breasts tipped with large pink nipples and they did that many times during the summer. His reason for being so fond of this position was her remark the first time they did it.

They were naked and she had sat on one of the dining room chairs as he stood before her and taken him in her mouth until he became stiff; then she stroked his erection until the lubricating nectar emerged from its tip. She added more of her saliva and stroked the moisture down its shaft and placed it between her breasts, pushing them together around his now pulsing sex. He began to gently thrust up and down in the moist narrow valley as her fingers caressed her nipples taut and upright.

He moaned softly and she laughed and murmured, "Ay, there's the rub."

II. MEMORIES

Fidel's Man in Portaria

(For Aphrodite Papastephanou)

THE GREEKS HAD SCHEDULED a national election that October we drove up from Delphi to Portaria in the mountains above the port of Volos. The parties conducted the campaign with ferocious enthusiasm. The communists promised themselves and the nation 17% of the vote and thought their chances were good. The phrase "KKE 17%" blossomed like a red flower on city walls and the massive mountains in the countryside. On the sheer cliffs along the twisting road to where the village hugs the green and brown mountain above the sea, the spray-can phrase pained the eye at regular intervals with its hopeful message. In the village, three hotels and a few tavernas surround the village square, small enough not to dwarf the villagers, but tall and broad enough to have acquired a certain age-stained dignity. After the chaos of Athens, the tourist-congested ruins of Delphi and the pocket metropolis of Volos, Portaria was idyllic. Only an exaggerated number of motor cars weaving among the goats and dogs on the narrow lanes intrusively reminded us of the technological-industrial age raging in the valley below. It was mid-September and only a few tourists could be seen clambering about the landscape.

The hotel in Delphi could have served as a house of horrors in a perverse amusement park and the long, sharply winding drive north had exhausted us. Our emotions snapped with an intense waspishness. Thus we felt a large measure of relief when the pretty hotel clerk said a room was free for us. Exhaustion began to transform itself into that muted exhilaration one feels when a place to sleep has been secured.

After registering and saluting our luck in the room with a stirrup cup of Greek brandy we wandered through the village before dinner. We walked slowly, allowing the village to seep into our minds. We wanted a glass of ouzo and a bit of quiet to talk desultorily about the rest of the trip and our experiences thus far.

We had forgotten the Greek passion for music and news broadcasts listened to at a volume just above the comfortable level. We sat at a table on the terrace of one of the smaller tavernas on the square. Only three other tables were occupied by local men whose conversation rose and fell in a rhythm we did not recognize. The alternating incongruous American pop music and incomprehensible news programs, piped through tinny loudspeakers onto the terrace, denied us the full measure of quiet we desired, but in spite of this we began to relax.

A short, round, energetic, man with a bright gold smile brought us a card on which the wares of the establishment were printed in blurred type. Since we would be eating dinner within the hour at the hotel, we ordered only two glasses of ouzo listed at 17 drachmas per glass. It was a good price and we liked the sharp anisette flavor of the clear liquid. The apparent owner of the place decided that these misguided foreigners would surely have trouble with the local aperativo. The source of this information remained a mystery. He spoke no English and we had too little Greek for a serious or any other kind of a discussion about food and drink. With many grand gestures and the repeated use of the word "prima" he made known to us that the ouzo for 17 drachmas was not nearly as good for us as the one noted on the menu card as "Extra." This item cost 80 drachmas. Not knowing his political affiliation at that point, we took his concern to be another example of capitalist greed. Still, if the stuff was indeed that much better, why not? It had been a long day. Agreed. Endaxi.

As the minutes that followed grew longer and longer we began to think the ouzo was so extra that he had to send out for it. But we had learned patience on this trip to the ancient Mediterranean cultures and smoked another cigarette. Soon the owner reappeared, balancing a large tray precariously on his upended arm. The contents of this tray surprised and astonished us. The "extra" was indeed that – it came in addition to the ouzo! A Minoan prince could not have asked for a more appetizing platter of various hors d'oeuvres: a small yellow omelet speckled with pieces of ham, cold sardines in oil, yogurt with onions, cold boiled potatoes, red beets, pieces of feta cheese, and some other items of unknown provenance along with two large chunks of local bread.

The ouzo arrived in a carafe accompanied by two shot glasses and the ubiquitous glasses of water. It was of course the 17-drachma variety, the only type he sold. After signing that we should enjoy our repast in the grand manner, he moved happily across the terrace. At the edge of it he joined a table of men in animated conversation under the leaves of a huge old plane tree. Lynn-Marie and I looked at each other with a mild sense of disbelief.

It was a typical situation: we did not want the damned stuff regardless of how good it might be; the dinner at the hotel was included in the price of the room. But equally we did not want to appear ungrateful even if we questioned the owner's motives. We thus wavered between the thought that he had merely wanted to ensure that the foreigners did not suffer any undue hardship from the effects of the strong local ouzo, a warm and friendly gesture common among the Greeks, and the idea that his base capitalist instincts had driven him to take advantage of the situation and give us more than we wanted, for which he would receive more than we intended to pay, a characteristic not entirely unknown in Greece. While we quietly debated the issue we sipped the ouzo and ate the food in bits and pieces. A multitude of exotic tastes filled our mouths with the flavors of the Greek landscape and the sea. Under the circumstances we preferred the former explanation of the owner's motives. Smiling, we sat enjoying the unordered bounty.

He must have been keeping an eye on us. When I pushed my plate away and started to light a cigarette he jumped up at his table and hurried in our direction waving a packet of his own brand. Standing over us he insisted we try one of his filtered brown paper cigarillos. Pointing to the packet he cried out, "Fidel Castro! Fidel Castro!"

Gesturing alternatively to himself and the cigarillos and pronouncing the words "Fidel Castro" a number of times, he clasped his hands together and raised his arms, allowing that not only was Fidel a great man, a strong, indeed a *maximum* leader, but that the two of them were great friends and that these very cigarillos which he smoked always came directly from his man in Havana. His face glowed with friendship and happiness at the thought. Surreptitiously I glanced around, looking for the red spray-painted phrase. It was nowhere to be seen. The owner's smile and enthusiasm shifted our opinion of his character. We said, "Evcharisto!" and nodded our agreement with his assessment of Fidel's character and the fine quality of the cigarillos, which tasted indeed just fine. After politely refusing one of our American cigarettes he went back to his friends under the plane tree, leaving us surrounded by an aura of comradely goodwill and sated hunger.

"How much do we dare to leave on the plates, I wonder?"

"I don't know. Even a little will be too much."

"We could skip dinner."

Our hotel was rated in the B class and the price had not been cheap.

By now darkness suffused the small square from which one could see the lights of Volos harbor in the distance. The village males promenaded around the street in front of us fingering their worry beads and crotches in the traditional Mediterranean manner, talking constantly of we knew not what, but guessed the general theme was politics and the election. The noisy radio in the taverna squawked the news and the men talked on in the expanding dusk. A half-dozen small children loudly played an obscure Greek children's game around the tables on the terrace.

We decided to pay and leave for the hotel, but the owner came over to present us with a small plate of freshly washed grapes. He looked at the uneaten food on our plates, which we considered negligible. Shaking his head and raising his eyebrows he signed to us his disappointment in our very un-Greek appetites. We smiled and shrugged sheepishly. The grapes tasted fine and we did our best to finish at least that part of the meal. We sipped the rest of the ouzo and did not give in to the urge to order another round. The mountain air had become chilled, but it remained fresh and clear.

The radio went off and three men walked across the square and the terrace into the taverna behind us. We grinned at each other, now full of knowledge about the local situation. Obviously a cell meeting of local party members! For a village this size we considered the cell rather large: the taverna owner with his mouth full of gold and friendly brown eyes, the others younger, leaner, hungrier.

One of the small children stopped scampering around the tables long enough to bring us our bill which the owner had written out in Greek on a scrap of paper. Lynn-Marie added up the tab and I got up to go into the taverna to pay it. One hundred seventy drachmas. My entrance interrupted the meeting in progress in the back of the main room. The men had plates of food similar to ours in front of them on the counter. They looked up blankly. The owner smiled. I gave him 200 drachmas and successfully protested when he tried to make change.

"Goodbye," he said in English.

"Yasaas," I said.

He laughed and shouted, "Viel Spass!" to which I replied briefly in German thanking him for his hospitality. If he did not understand all the words, I think he knew what I meant. He nodded and smiled.

We walked slowly through the darkness down the narrow streets to the hotel, enjoying the smells of the village and the tiny lights of the houses scattered about the mountainside. The Greeks were so friendly in those villages. We wanted to stay longer, but were expected elsewhere and could not break the schedule.

The dinner in the antiseptic hotel dining room made us regret not remaining at the taverna. We did not return to the square the next day to photograph the place and its owner. We never did learn its name; perhaps it had none. We hoped his disappointment was not great when the KKE received only eleven percent in the election.

(Athens, 1981)

55

A Weekend Trip to Port of Sète on the Mediterranean Sea: A Preface and a Letter

A Brief Prefatory Note.

IN THE LATE SPRING OF 1980, Lynn-Marie and I drove from Paris to Sitges, a beach town south of Barcelona not then as yet discovered by the international homosexual community. We planned to spend several nights in various places on the coast while driving to Spain. The first stop was in Avignon whose sun-blasted beige Palace of the Popes dominates the Rhône river and the bridge under (or on) which one legendarily dances. Neither of us had been there previously, but we would spend a great deal of time there in the following decades.

Early the next morning, having retrieved our rental car from the courtyard of the Palace where we had illegally parked it, we drove south to the Saintes-Maries-de-la-mer, formerly a small fishing village that had captured the attention of van Gogh, Aldington, Mistral and Durrell, among others, and we wished to know why. We had not thought to telephone ahead to make a room reservation, thinking that our off-season trip would not require such a precaution. As Puck once famously commented, "Lord, what fools these mortals be!" As we drove through the Camargue we began to notice an increasing amount of traffic heading in the same direction on the narrow, two-lane road. A few kilometers outside the town, traffic came to a stumbling halt. A hotel room? We could barely enter the town. We had chosen, innocently of course when innocence is the same as ignorance, the very weekend of the annual spring Roma (gypsy) festival that brings thousands of visitors to the area, clogging the roads, and filling the hotels and inns to capacity and beyond.

Eventually we inched our way into a parking space, ate a hasty not very satisfactory lunch, and painfully drove through the morass of people and vehicles back north out of the Camargue to the next road going west along the coast, thinking we would find a room in the next town and continue the journey the following day. Ignorant innocence? Innocent ignorance? C'est la même chose, n'est-ce pas?

To mercifully shorten the story, at 9:30 that evening, almost out of gas, tired, cranky and hungry, we drove into the thoroughfare leading into the seaport called Sète and saw before us the stately edifice on the canal festooned with balconies jutting out from the façade, just deep enough to hold two people with their glasses of calvados. The large, brightly lighted sign read, LE

GRAND HOTEL, and, now willing to pay any price, we dared to hope we might find shelter for the night and a decent dinner. And grand the hotel was, and possibly still is, a luxurious haven in which to recover from the tribulations of a long arduous day. We returned to Sète twice over the years, the time described below and once much later with brother Dean, to whom the following letter is addressed and who has worked in various capacities for two decades at the Wentworth-by-the-Sea resort hotel in Portsmouth, New Hampshire; thus the greeting that heads the letter. The late Georges Brassens (1921-1981), un génie sans doute, is a self-described pornographer of the phonograph and rascal of song.

("J'suis l'pornographe / du phonographe / le polisson / de la chanson")

Brassens was born, grew up and is buried in Sète. Tavel is a small village 17 kilometers northwest of Avignon where Lynn-Marie and I lived for a year in 1982-83.

This brief introduction should, I hope, serve to clarify certain understandable obscurities in the text, and for those that remain helpful footnotes have been provided.

Key West, December 2004

Dear Wentworthist,

As a warm-up exercise[1] I thought I'd briefly tell you about the trip to Sète we made last weekend. It was something of the spur of the moment, both of us hoping that the overcast and fog would lift as we neared the coast. Silly thought to have entertained. We drove down the west side of the Rhône, the wrong side because of the electricity generating plants and other disruptions of the landscape on that bank of the river. Our first stop was Aigues-Mortes, a walled town we had visited in 1980, or so we had repeatedly informed people, but when we arrived at the gate next to the Constance Tower the dark suspicion began to form in my brain that I'd never seen this place before. Walking through the gate and down the street leading to the Place St. Louis, the social if not geographic center of the town, past the vegetable stalls and bistros and Louis' small medieval church from which he left on his own private crusade to smash the infidel in the Holy Lands, the suspicion hardened into the uncomfortably true fact that this town had no canals running through it, which is how we remembered it in 1980. We had, in fact,

---

[1]Like many writers, when I was younger I often found that writing a letter or two got me started at the pen and paper, or typewriter, after which I could better move forward with the more creative efforts.

never set foot in the place. It had been Grau du Roi, a few kilometers further west down the coast where we had eaten that small slice of pizza and searched unsuccessfully for a hotel room, not Aigues-Mortes at all. So one learns.

After walking all over the tightly confined quarters of this fortified burg in the middle of a swamp (dead waters is right, though in Louis' day the sea came right up to the edge of the walls), taking notes for the story of a dying poet,[2] we bought four grapefruits and returned to the car and headed off to – Grau du Roi, of course. We did not stop there, but drove through it to add the final clincher regarding our whereabouts three years earlier in sunnier weather. Some 20 kilometers before Sète we stopped the car and climbed over the dunes with our picnic basket complete with cheese, sausage, the inevitable baguette, beach blanket (actually a red-white-blue sheet upon which the wind spilled vin blanc) and copy of the latest *Paris-Match*. We were able to finish lunch and the wine before the fog separated us from the sea and the rest of the beachscape as well. No sunbathing, topless or otherwise.

After a couple of wrong turns in Sète (after all, we'd been there on that route at night before and had enjoyed very good luck) the five floors of the Grand Hotel loomed over the Canal Royal in front of us. We knew there would be no problem with

---

[2]See "Dead Waters" elsewhere in this volume.

getting a room facing the canal because we found a parking space for the car directly across the street from the hotel entrance. And this turned out to be the case.

Standing on the balcony of our room overlooking the canal, sipping fruity calvados from our own glasses (purchased in the Monoprix department store in Chartres on the first trip to France and taken with us on our travels since then) surrounded by the décor of a turn of the century New Orleans bordello, as I never tire of repeating, we imagined Brassens as a pimply youth scurrying about below trying to impress his girl friend with a new poem. We suddenly did not mind the fact that we could hardly see to the other side of the canal, so thick had the fog become. We laughed and decided to investigate more of the town than had been possible last time.

The calvados and the fog made us restless. Late Saturday afternoon is a busy time in a port, even when the dockworkers are on strike and the boats are forced to detour to Marseille to indifferently unload freight and tourists alike onto the wharf. We walked for a long time in the crowds of shoppers and striking workers who rolled from side to side with each step as if compensating for the roll of the ship. We shivered occasionally as the gray cold penetrated our spring clothing, purchased cigarettes, a local newspaper and the *International Herald Tribune*, and sat at a café on the canal to drink beer and read the headlines. Can't recall what the subjects were, but no doubt they were important to different audiences.

Having absorbed sufficient headline knowledge for the moment, we walked along the row of seafood restaurants that line the canal, trying unsuccessfully to remember in which one we had eaten three summers ago. One really ought to write things like that down in a small pocket notebook without which one does not travel. After deciding on one of them (for a now forgotten reason, they all looked pretty much the same and served pretty much the same fare), we retired to the hotel and a brief nap and a short nip of calvados. The room had become uncomfortably chilly and I knocked on the radiator with my shoe (the traditional Sètoise method of eliciting heat from a recalcitrant furnace), which brought no relief so we left and went to the restaurant earlier than anticipated. This did not matter since we had not made a reservation.

The dinner will long remain in my memory as indicative of how well the unknown can taste. One entire course remains a mystery to both of us, although we suspect it consisted of chunks of octopus bathed in a sharp cream sauce of local manufacture. This does not mean we did not like it, simply that we really don't know exactly what it was. My oysters were not the bi-valve I've come to know and love: much too small and tasteless. However, my sole meunière was the best of that dish I have ever eaten. Lynn-Marie's poisson du jour, whatever it may have been, was almost as good. The two wines, both local and white, provided a fine and tasty balance to the food. (One would be forgiven for thinking we could not read the menu correctly; this is only partially true, some of the dishes were described in a vernacular that even Parisians would find difficult to decipher.) After a while I even forgot the restaurant staff refused to shut the door to the cold fog exterior and by the time we ordered the espresso my biology had acclimated itself to a comfortable level. Back at the bordello we drank a final calvados and slept well.

The room, if not the world outside, warmed up during the night, making a shower possible, the first since Paris! This statement should not lead to the conclusion that we do not bathe regularly; it does mean that our rented house in Tavel boasts only a bathtub and a hand shower; not quite the same thing as a stand-up shower. One of the highlights of staying at Le Grand Hôtel is eating breakfast in the bright, tall atrium filled with live green plants, throughout which plastic flowers are interspersed, and aging but well-dressed French men and women doing what they do best, enjoying life while complaining about everything that they encounter. Usually the atrium is ablaze with sunlight; this time, however, it glowed dully with the pale light of seafog.

Nonetheless, we ate with good appetite the croissant and pieces of baguette loaded with marmalade and savored the professionally made, as opposed to our own amateur efforts, café au lait in large French bowls. After checking out of the hotel we drove directly to the Cimetière Marin and this time asked the caretaker exactly where the tombe de Valéry was located; no walking about the place for an hour without finding it like the last time. Without consulting his location guide (do so many visitors ask about this grave?) he told us and we found it without delay: a modest family marble slab with a small headstone, his name on one side of the slab amidst the names of other family members. Unless one already knew who he was, one would not know from the tombstone that here lies one of the great French poets and intellectuals of the 20th century. The same simplicity adorns Jean Vilar's family tomb in the same cemetery, his name simply one of many on the marble. From this one would not know how important this creative giant was to the history of postwar French theater.

Further along the coast we found the Cimetière du Py (locally known as the Cemetery of the Poor, though it lies on the shore of the Mediterranean!) and the brand new grave of Georges Brassens, his name engraved in the lower left hand corner of the headstone.[3] The Brassens section of the Valéry Museum not far from the cemetery is rather large and the first thing one encounters is a videotape loop of some of his recent appearances on television shows. From the few minutes I saw of it one can safely ignore the screen and move on. The rest of the permanent exhibition consists of a large collection of letters written for the museum by famous friends after his death (such as Tino Rossi, Charles Trenet, Patachou, Les Frères Jacques, and the like), all reminiscing about better days or written directly to the now dead Brassens bemoaning his leaving them while he was so young ... Disgusting stuff accompanied by large photographs of the letter writers usually in the company of Brassens. If I find the time I may write a letter of protest to the museum director. Merde. Otherwise, the usual stuff devoted to individuals who create marvelous things, become popular and eventually bite the dust: one of his pipes with pipe cleaner, eyeglasses, loads of manuscripts, copies of his books, his recordings, contracts, posters advertising his concerts and

---

[3] Brassens has a sarcastic song about cemeteries that begins, "J'ai des tombeaux en abondance/des sépultur's à discretion/dans tout cim'tière d' quelque importance." For the rest of the text, as well as the text to "Le pornographe" and many of his other songs, see Alphonse Bonnafé, *Georges Brassens* (Paris: Éditions Seghers, 1963).

masses of photographs, much of which is of real interest.[4]

Since our time was running short, we made a cursory foray through the Valéry section to note that nothing had been added or subtracted since our last visit (during which I closely examined everything for more than an hour). Once again I was impressed by his drawing and watercolor talents. Renewed my inspiration in this direction and since then I've taken up abstract watercolors. The widow of the painter François Desnoyer has given the museum a great number of his works in oil, watercolor, gouache, and pencil, all of which are now displayed on the second floor balcony (but not his portrait of Brassens, interestingly enough) and are worth contemplating for a while – lots of glorious color splashed about with apparent abandon on scenes of the coast and the towns of Provence. You know, however, that they are surely very well thought out, especially when you see some of his studies for them with their mathematically precise plotted graphs of lines controlling the balance of the works.

We bought a Sète baguette, sausage and a bottle of red wine before we rolled out of town, thinking to eat on the road if the fog lifted and if we found

---

[4]Brassens now has his own museum, Espace Georges Brassens, in a different part of the town, and these days apparently one can eat at a restaurant called Les Amis de Georges, apparently named after the eponymous song written by the singer Moustaki. There is no escape from the commercial instinct.

an appropriate corner in the landscape. Consequently, we did not drive on the autoroute, but stayed on the smaller roads leading to Sommières and Nîmes, the former of which we wanted to see on the way back to Tavel; for one thing Durrell lives there and the ancient Romans built the bridge over the Vidourle river, so it must be interesting, n'est-ce pas? We arrived in the town of about 4000 at midday and walked through the narrow medieval streets with Renaissance arcades and façades and squares, searching for an interesting restaurant at our price level. Since we found only a small pizzeria and a hotel restaurant that was full, we drove out along the river and parked near the arena where we picnicked on the riverbank, smiling often for no evident reason, swallowing with great pleasure the red wine, biting into the green pepper sausage (saucisson poivre vert), thrilling at the tiny explosion of the peppercorn's sharp tang before it faded into the general flavor of garlic and pork.

Thinking that it would be fun to return one Sunday afternoon this summer to watch the cours libre[5] or a Spanish bullfight, we drove slowly out

---

[5]The Provençal version of the contest is bloodless and involves the human contestants, inevitably young men in white clothes and red bandanas with a small hook in one hand, running across the bull's path attempting to snatch a rosette from the string stretched between the bull's horns. If anyone gets hurt it is the young men. Aficionados of the Spanish version distain this one as being effete.

of the town toward home, happy in the knowledge that a Krimi[6] would be on the television that night.[7]

Several hours interruption here. A plot for a story occurred to me and I wrote out some notes and the first six pages of a tale about a thief on the run and the chapel of the gray penitents on the rue des Teinturiers (the street of the cloth dyers) in the quarter of the same name in Avignon. I've been to the chapel twice and will go once more to ensure I've got the topography right.[8] Some progress on volume II of the Berlin novel can also be reported, but I am seriously considering recasting the entire thing (about 100 pages of typescript so far); this will require adjustments to volume one as well. The whole thing has to be tightened and given some internal structure that is presently lacking. It is all somewhat confusing, but necessary before I go on much further.[9]

---

[6]"Krimi" is a shortened version of the German word "Kriminalgeschichte," or criminal story.

[7]We did not return to Sommières that year, though I had briefly corresponded with Durrell some months earlier. In fact, we did not go back to the town until 1992, when the International Lawrence Durrell Society met in Avignon and arranged an excursion to the writer's house to drink wine, eat hors d'oeurvres and listen to the editor of Durrell's collected poem, James Brigham, recite some of them. Unfortunately, the author had died two years earlier, so our brief meeting at the university in College Station, Pennsylvania in 1986 remains our only meeting.

[8]See the story, "No Refuge for a Sinner" elsewhere in this volume.

[9]After neglecting the unfinished manuscript of the second volume of the Berlin novel for 15 years, I returned to it four years ago. The current structure of the project is a five-volume epic that I may live to finish. Volume I has been completely rewritten, volumes II and III are

A mistral began to howl early this morning, maddening both man and beast, but washing the overcast out of the sky, bringing a return of the bright southern sun and dropping the temperature to unacceptably cold levels. I plan to importune the gods tonight on the balcony with an offering of Finette's entrails. This wind-crazed hound cornered a strange cat underneath a large bush below our living room window in the courtyard. With a constant stream of hysterical yelps the frantic terrier darted in and out of the bush creating a godawful barrage of noise. This cat, however, was not to be buffaloed, as it were, and when Finette's piercing yowls rose a few decibels I knew without getting out of my chair that the puss had struck back. Suddenly, puss made a break into the nether reaches of the garden followed by Finette whose howling now reached a banshee level, overwhelming even the mistral's screaming. Beside herself with emotions unknown to mere humans, the little monster leaped in the air, ran in circles, jumped up the garage wall, screaming at a painfully intense pitch until the cat somehow eluded its tormentor. At least I think so. As I write this I hear odd hissing noises from below, but Finette is not responding. Perhaps the cat

in various stages of completion and notes exist for the following two. There is no limit on the ambition of some writers.

successfully scratched the dog's nose. We may never know.[10]

Yours in faith,
B.

---

[10]The uncontrollable hysterical terrier belonged to our lovely old landlady, Madame Mourre, a native Taveloise, who no doubt had been given the hound as a present and did not wish to insult the giver by sending the mutt to its well-deserved end in doggy heaven, or hell in this case. Anything could, and did, set the unbalanced canine off its head and into a rage of yelping unequalled in dogdom except by those demented Chihuahuas leaping up and down pissing in spurts on the rug. Less that a year after we left Tavel, Madame Mourre died, an event that caused us deep sadness, and, we can assume, Finette was appropriately taken care of.

Gunsmoke and Provençal Pizza Sundays (A Cowboy Culinary, Euro-American Adventure)

(For the late John Hickman, the very much alive Ed Walker, and American University's WAMU radio program *The Big Broadcast*.)

SUNDAYS ARE NOT SUNDAYS IN THE SUMMER in the same way Sundays are Sundays in the autumn-winter-springtime.

Summer Sundays are too hot and humid for the kitchen stove at 500 degrees Fahrenheit and there is no brick stone and mortar oven in the patio down from the kitchen back near the giant goldfish.

Not with us in Washington DC there isn't.

So Sundays in the summer in Washington chez nous are not real Sundays but only partially complete Sundays because complete Sundays must end with sizzling Provençal pizza made between seven o'clock and eight o'clock in the evening listening to *The Great Gildersleeve* and *Nightbeat* and *The Lone Ranger* and *Lum and Abner* and slowly magnificently consumed with knife and fork at eight o'clock accompanied by the little moral tales of U.S. Marshall Matt Dillon, and Doc, Chester and Kitty, metaphysical tales in which the dualism of good and evil plays out in stories with all too human ambiguity.

Listening to *The Big Broadcast*, four hours of "old time radio," is a requirement and part of the definition of a complete Sunday.

Aromawhelming pizza made lovingly in a 500 degree Fahrenheit dry hot oven on a pizza stone already heated for an hour prior to receiving the Sunday offering, to hold it hotly for ten seared minutes, no more but little less, ten being the magic number for this Provençal pizza, dusted with herbes de Provence. This pizza can now be superlatively made by only one person, my own Lynn-Marie, since several years ago the inimitable François, that small, grinning Sicilian, mysteriously left the Barthelasse island in the Rhône river by Avignon for parts unknown, a small but wiry *French* Sicilian, he always insisted, as he insisted on his being related to Frank Sinatra: "Il a une maman italienne, moi, j'ai une maman italienne, alors!" Lynn-Marie is not Sicilian, although she has an Italian mother, and is thus, in François's terms, related to Frank Sinatra and to him. Nevertheless, she is the only one who can create the French Sicilian's Provençal pizza.

The answer for François was as simple and as happy as his character when he shoved the smallish, extremely thin-crusted pizza into the wood-burning stone and mortar oven, always skeptical that one bubbling and popping Provençal pizza, a vinaigrette salad, and a bottle of local dry red wine constituted a sufficient amount of food to render us visibly, beamingly ecstatic. "You don't wish any pasta course?"

And after his unexplained departure, new tenants broke the Sicilian's red-tiled roof pizza restaurant into a pale beige Tex-Mex chain-and-leather-French-Italian series of successively alienating renovations to distress and disappoint us. Just across the river sits the pale yellow Palace of the Popes, and if they could know about it, they would certainly look askance and also be depressed by this sorrowful turn of events.

Memory's gauze curtains of the mind confuse the origins of this curious association combining pizza of the Midi, bubbling and popping gruyère fromage, homemade tomato sauce, garlic, jambon, garlic, and garlic, with the farrago of private eyes, extraterrestrials, jesters, big band swing, and cowboys on parade on the air, all this dazzling congruence of American sounds and Mediterranean tastes.

Out of mysterious, mist-shrouded beginnings suddenly Sundays became Sundays with sharply gurgling spiced olive-oiled Provençal pizza, darkened with cooking heat, bursting on the taste-centers, filling the cranium with vertiginous transcendence, and lifting the belly to the stratosphere of delights, washed gently but firmly with rosé de Tavel or Napa Valley merlot into a state of satisfaction unknown to humankind since Lucullus finished his last meal with a cosmic sigh.

This edenic stage of existence remains incomplete without its other, electronic, component.

Food for the body, metaphysics for the mind.

The bridge across the ocean: the traditions of the wind-swept high plains full of violence and pain, and the wine-and-sun-soaked troubadour of western love: the cool American psychology-bedeviled consciousness attempting to engorge the warm Mediterranean landscape of silvery olive trees and sudden climate changes: the hard rain falls on Dodge City decaying the soul, the mistral whips the countryside around Avignon cleaning the air to make the brain hum with thoughts of suicide.

On Sunday evenings the opposites duel to a draw for Monday mornings.

Lucullus, le pauvre, had no radio to transport his mind with little moral tales: he thought them up himself, and they pleased him more than guests at his table.

So, for us, summer Sundays remain incomplete because at eight o'clock we still eat with *Gunsmoke* after disagreeing about *Lum and Abner*, but we do not eat bopping, savory-snazzling Provençal pizza regularly on summer Sundays, alas.

Which is unfortunate and regrettable, but inadequate air-conditioning disallows 500 degree

Fahrenheit ovens in Washington on summer Sundays, or any other summer days, but especially on summer Sundays because Sundays simply are pizza days, Provençal thin-crusted herbes de Provence tomato garlic shredded gruyère copasetic capacolla pizza days, and they are peculiarly ours. Ergo, we must doubtlessly build a brick stone and mortar over for the backyard near the giant goldfish before they are too old and deaf and die, because they too listen to *Gunsmoke*, we think, and we feed them their own delightful morsels, about which we think they are delighted: at least the two ancient fish-friends, one blind and the other over-weight, slurf the morsels down with astonishing speed.

And *Gunsmoke* is Sunday night at eight o'clock with a mouthful of flavor of dry red wine and of thin herbes de Provence garlic pizza on the Fahrenheit 500 degree stone and in our watering mouths.

That is the definition of Sunday evening, but not in the summer in Washington, which leads ineluctably to two possible modalities of resolution: move to northern Minnesota with a trunk-full of tapes, or build the brick stone and mortar oven in the backyard near the giant but aging goldfish so Sundays will be complete even in the summer.

(Washington, August 1999)

75

Addendum 2001:

We no longer need to think of building the oven in the backyard near the fish for summer Sundays since we had central air conditioning installed a year ago. And we no longer need a trunk-full of tapes because we now have a set of speakers attached to the computer, which will allow us to listen to the show in real time through the Internet no matter where we are on the East coast of the country. Unfortunately, we will have a problem if we move to France or Italy because the show will run from 1:00 AM to 5:00 AM given the time changes. We could, of course, shift our sleeping arrangements around to accommodate the "real time" presentation, and eating pizza at two in the morning is not unheard of in some circles. But under those circumstances there is one inescapable fact: *Gunsmoke* and provençal pizza will happen on Mondays.

Addendum 2002:

The mysterious marvels of enveloping computer technology have once again pushed the mundane frontiers of the possible even further. We now live in Key West, out in the Gulf of Mexico along the Straits of Florida ninety miles from Cuba, but we still listen to *The Big Broadcast* and *Gunsmoke*, though not necessarily on Sunday nights. Social and business schedules often preclude the Sunday tradition, but now the broadcast is "archived" for a week after Sunday so one can listen to it whenever one wishes. Another change not so felicitous is the heat in this tropical climate: running the oven at 500 degrees for an hour is often not the best way to spend any evening, so we order a thin-crust pizza to be delivered and "doctor" it to our satisfaction, extra garlic and a fistful of herbes de provence. O yes. Not quite the same, but close enough.

To quote the great Count Basie: "One more time," 2003:

A new house, centrally air-conditioned, has rendered us capable of once again making our own pizza whilst listening to *The Big Broadcast* any day or night of the week.

Ah, Paradise, regained!

Thinking of Durrell in Key West

This is not Sommières
Nor was it meant to be
But it may be as close
As I will ever come
  To living there:

Mediterranean temperament
Point de vue caraïbe, tu sais.

The winds of passion blow
Across the floating mangroves
As over the boules court on the
  Vidourle.

We have neither of us come home
But we will make do
  For now.

20.VIII.2002

Brief Impressions of Egypt and Greece:
A 1996 Letter

(For Soad Sobhy, in memoriam)

Washington DC, July 1996

Dear Friends,

Since so many have expressed an interest in hearing about our recent trip to Egypt and Greece, but since so few have the time or energy to actually listen, in person, to the telling about the journey, several have asked if I intend to perhaps write something about it, which they could then pursue at their leisure, when they might find any. So I have scribbled down, so to speak, a brief narrative of this series of interconnected events, which may, in fact, give some pleasure to them what reads it, as Lord Johnnie said to the disheveled archbishop just after tea on what threatened to be a fateful day at Newgate Calendar.

Two compelling reasons motivated the trip: participation in the academic literary conference entitled On Miracle Ground IX in Alexandria, Egypt, the ninth conference of that title organized by the International Lawrence Durrell Society

(ILDS), of which Lynn-Marie and I are members in good standing, and to see our Athenian friends whom we'd not seen in many years.

One would be forgiven for at first thinking the ILDS to be what is commonly known in Hollywood and the world of popular music as a "fan club," the etymology of which no doubt can be traced to the word "fanatic." Indeed, there are similarities, it must be admitted, but no simple fan club has to my knowledge regularly published an academic journal (*Deus Loci*, in this case), nor organized academic conferences the papers of which are published in a series of "proceedings." The ILDS does, it is true, publish a fans' newsletter (*The Herald*).[11]

Some years ago the Society's equivalent to an "executive committee" decided to hold every other bi-annual conference outside North America. In 1992, the Society arranged the conference in the Palais des Papes in the walled and fabled city of Avignon, a locale which gave its name to Durrell's last major work, *The Avignon Quintet*.[12] Having gotten its feet wet in foreign waters,[13] as it were,

---

[11] Founded and edited by Susan Stiers MacNiven until her untimely death in 2003 robbed us of a much-beloved colleague and friend.

[12] This "quincunx" of novels consists of *Monsieur* (1974), *Livia, Or Buried Alive* (1978), *Constance, or Solitary Practices* (1982), *Sebastian, or Ruling Passions* (1983), and *Quinx, or The Ripper's Tale* (1985).

[13] The conference was, in fact, very well watered (trés bien arrosé) thanks to the preparations organized by Denis Constancias, which

the Society decided to hold the 1996 conference in Alexandria, the locus of Durrell's famous *Alexandria Quartet* (made up of the novels *Justine, Balthazar, Mountolive,* and *Clea,* published between 1957 and 1960). Where else, after all, could be more appropriate to consider all the possible aspects, obscure and blatant, of *The Quartet* than in its own city?

Alexandria

Scheduled for five days, thus surely making it one of the longest academic conferences devoted to a single subject on record, the series of events at and surrounding the gathering proved to be thrilling, exciting, exhausting, satisfying, and worth the expense, the heat, the lunatic taxi drivers, and the illness that affects all but the most hearty European digestive system when visiting the Middle East and Africa, what the Egyptians call, not without a certain dose of Schadenfreude, the "pharaoh's revenge," no doubt to redress to a small degree the theft of so many Egyptian treasures by Euro-centric archeologists and their patrons (with the connivance, it must be admitted, of certain venal Egyptian officials), but this is speculation.

---

included arranging for local wineries to donate samples of their production.

Those special women and men of the University of Alexandria, faculty and students, clearly spent a vast amount of time and energy organizing the events surrounding the conference panels, at many of the latter of which they also read papers.[14] All of us appreciated, and indeed needed, this support in that for most of us strange and rather alien culture.

The quality of the papers themselves ranged over the usual spectrum of such things: ca. 20% can be described as brilliant, ca. 20% can be written off as at best inadequate, and the rest fall somewhere in the middle. This is quite normal for any academic conference. What could most assuredly not be described as normal for most of us was the setting.

Alexandria is, alas, no longer what it once was. While apparently always somewhat dusty, and in the first half of the 20th century even somewhat shabby at the edges, after 1956 and the spate of Arab nationalization that followed,[15] the city

---

[14]The best of the papers were to be published as conference proceedings under the editorship of Professor Soad Hussein Sobhy, who was a member of the University of Alexandria faculty and served as the local coordinator of the event. To everyone's sorrow, Dr. Sobhy was diagnosed with cancer and spent the brief remainder of her life fighting the disease in various hospitals and clinics in Egypt, Europe and the United States. The proceedings have not been published (2004).

[15]The Egyptian nationalization of the Suez Canal led to the unfortunate war of that name when the British, the French and the Israelis invaded Egypt intending to reverse that decision, an incompletely thought through move undermined by the US government's overt hostility

radically altered in the process of transforming itself into an Arab city rather than what it had once been: a minor thriving cosmopolitan commercial and cultural center, enjoying a balance of European and Arab (Egyptian) influences that apparently made it livable for both its European minority and its Egyptian citizens.

Indeed, there is evidence, subjective to be sure, that the process began long before 1956. Gwyn Williams, who lived in the city during and after the war, has written the following eulogy for the Alexandria that had started to mutate even in 1942-1945 under the crushing pressures of the war.

> It had never been an Egyptian city, and for the Romans it had been not Alexandria in Egypt but Alexandria ad Aegyptum. The city was being Egyptianized, not from the working class Egyptian quarter but from official Cairo. European street and quarter names were changed ... It had been a city of Italians, Greeks, Syrians, Lebanese, European Jews and Jews of native origin, with a culture we might dub Edwardian but with its center and resort of cultural refreshment in Paris. All this I felt was being rolled into the sea.[16]

toward the project. The invaders, humiliated, retreated, and the Egyptians increased the intensity of their nationalization program, in effect driving the remaining Europeans out of the country, with or without their property.

[16] "Durrell in Egypt" in *Twentieth Century Literature*, vol 3, no. 3 (Fall, 1987), 301. European attitudes and opinions regarding the city have recently come under criticism for their biases by Arab writers, especially after the latter absorbed the lessons in the late Edward Said's seminal *Orientalism* (1978) and *Cultural Imperialism* (1993). See for example, Khaled Fahmy, "For Cavafy, with Love and Squalor: Some

Today, the non-Arab population of the city's European and Jewish cemeteries is immensely larger than the tiny number of such people who live in the city. Consequently, one of the main results of national independence for Egypt has been the egyptianization of the city, that is to say the deliberate erasure of those cosmopolitan elements (read: European, esp. Greek and British), which made the place unique, interesting, and worth living in, not only for the European Alexandrians, but for the Egyptians as well. In short, the Egyptian city is no longer Durrell's, E.M. Forster's, or Constantine Cavafy's city, indeed there is some evidence that it is no longer even the Egyptian novelist Naguib Mahfouz' city.[17] (And in

---

Critical Notes on the History and Historiography of Modern Alexandria" in Anthony Hirst & Michael Silk (eds.), *Alexandria, Real and Imagined* (London, 2004), 263-280, and Azza Kararah, "Egyptian Literary Images of Alexandria" in ibid., 307-321. Soad Sobhy's "The Fabulator's Perspective on Egypt in *The Alexandria Quartet*" in *Deus Loci*, NS 4 (1995-96), 85-96, is an earlier investigation of this subject well worth reading.

[17]Durrell lived there from 1943 to 1945. The details of Durrell's life are to be found in Ian MacNiven's standard *Lawrence Durrell. A Biography* (London & New York, 1998) and the revised edition of Gordon Bowker's *Through the Dark Labyrinth: A Biography of Lawrence Durrell* (London, 1998); Forster lived there during the 1914-18 bloodletting in Europe, working for the Red Cross and gathering impressions he would later put into his book *Alexandria. A History and a Guide* (still in print), which Durrell used to good effect when writing *The Quartet;* the poet Cavafy (1863-1933) lived most of his life in the city, about which he wrote so many brilliant, achingly human poems. The most evident Mahfouz work on the city is the interestingly

fact it never was the Europeans' city; they always and ever formed a small minority of the population in the last two centuries up to the mid-1950s.)

Today the European must accustom himself to the dust, the heat, the importuning of people of all ages wishing to transact some form of business in the exchange of which they will increase their incomes and the European might increase his pleasure in the city, and the truly incredible comically shattering noise of motor vehicle horns. Other than Cairo, Alexandria is possibly the noisiest city in the world since motor vehicle klaxons are the favorite instruments upon which Egyptians play *all the time day and night and forever after.* Or so it would seem, although at 5.30 one morning one could almost hear the harbor water lapping up to the Corniche wall. Indeed, the relative quiet of the early morning sunrise hours in Alexandria is a vast contrast to the rest of the day-night with its constant super volume of bleating noise and traffic chaos.

The participants found rooms at the Cecil Hotel (the site of the conference's headquarters) and the Metropole, still under renovation across the square. The opening sessions were held at the University, to which a bus took us from the hotels. If the first apprehension of the city's sights and sounds had not been sufficient to knock some of us off our

---

structured novel, so similar to Durrell's experiment with time and space in The *Quartet*, but not nearly as long, *Miramar* (1967).

complacently "first-world" perch, the sight of the security guards, one of whom was armed with what seemed to me to be a reasonable facsimile of a machine gun (probably not an Uzi), climbing onto the bus surely shook some of the perch's foundation. The guards accompanied us wherever we traveled as a group on the bus. Our Egyptian hosts obviously suffered with concerns beyond those our homegrown academics normally have to worry about when planning a conference.

If one describes the variety of participants in and attendees at the conference, one is sorely tempted to simply say "all the usual suspects, several new Europeans and North Americans, and a dozen or so Egyptians." But this would not at all indicate that one of the "usual suspects" is a retired English teacher lady from Kyoto who also attended the conference in Avignon (the Middle East must have come as quite a shock to her and her companion), that another is a researcher from the Gennadis Library in Athens (an American, I believe), and that others come from places as far apart as the Bronx and Dublin and Vancouver. Nor would that simple statement tell you that one of the first-timers came from Moscow, another from Cyprus (a Scot), a third Memphis (Tennessee), and a fourth from an obscure college in Ohio. And, finally, such a description would not by any means inform you that the Alexandrian and Cairene women academics of all ages at the conference do a quite credible variation on the traditional belly dance. A wonderfully motley crew.

A few words about the hotels. The Cecil is air-conditioned, an important consideration for summer guests regardless of ethnicity. Opened in 1930, it immediately became *the* hotel for visiting European of certain means. Recent renovations have retained its original charm and style in the lobby and the hallways with their great expanses of mirrors, including an ancient dual elevator that may or may not work at any given time, but is serviced by two large but friendly lift-operators. The rooms facing the sea and Zaad Zaghloul Square, directly opposite the building, are to be preferred for the view, but not the noise. Some of the rooms seem to have escaped much of the renovation efforts, but still, when in Alexandria one might as well stay at the city's grand old hotel, an institution which makes appearances in *The Quartet* ("In the gaunt lounge of the Cecil Hotel she [Justine] would perhaps be waiting, gloved hands folded on her handbag, staring out through the windows upon which the sea crawled and sprawled, climbing and subsiding, across the screen of palms in the little municipal square which flapped and creaked like loose sails," is an often cited passage),[18] *Miramar* ("I have paid a

---

[18] Lawrence Durrell, *The Alexandria Quartet* (in one volume, London, 1962), 550 (*Mountolive*). The square is no longer little, though it may

nostalgic visit to Athineos, Pastroudis and the Antoniadis Gardens, and I have sat for some time in the lobbies of the Cecil and the Windsor, the places where pashas and foreign politicians used to meet in the old days"),[19] and possibly other works of literature as yet unread by me. The rooms at the Cecil are not inexpensive, but those of us who stayed there thoroughly enjoyed the proximity of the lecture rooms to the bar. In fact, when we decided to skip the afternoon sessions, we sat in the bar with friends and drank European wine and chewed salted peanuts and ate an occasional fly that happened to light on one's lip and was swallowed with a gulp of the imported red, as our good friend Richard Pine discovered one blazingly bright afternoon as we debated the relative merits of two academics' "investigations" of love in the Quartet.[20] Needless to say we came to no

---

still be municipal; it is now a vast plot of urban park, always crowded, which marches down to the Corniche and the majestic vista of the harbor. The Cecil plays a role throughout all four volumes; a representative sampling would be: "They met where I had first seen her, in the gaunt vestibule of the Cecil Hotel, in a mirror." (58, *Justine*), "I see her [Justine] ... in the vestibule of the Cecil Hotel, among the dusty palms ..." (23, *Justine*), and "They met more than once, formally, like business partners, in the lounge of the Cecil Hotel to discuss the matter of this marriage with the detachment of Alexandrian brokers planning a cotton merger. This is the way of the city." (245, *Balthazar*)

[19]Naguib Mahfouz, *Miramar* (Cairo, 1978), 12.

[20]Richard Pine is the notorious author of the standard study of Lawrence Durrell's works, *The Mindscape* (2nd revised edition Corfu, 2005), something of a companion to Ian MacNiven's biography, and other literary studies. He is also the founder of the Durrell School of Corfu and its Academic Director.

conclusion, but we *so* enjoyed the talk – and the wine!

The prices at the renovation-work-in-progress Metropole, obliquely across the square at a right angle from the Cecil, are not so expensive, and the lack of air conditioning is somewhat compensated for by the sea breezes that blow through the rooms facing the harbor. The view is magnificent, but also overlooks the tram station, so the noise level is high. The rooms have high ceilings and large bathrooms and are appointed with old wood furniture. Our colleagues who stayed here noted with smiles that each day some new piece of the building would appear as workers removed curtains and scaffolding covering the on-going renovation. We ate lunch in the hotel's more or less air conditioned restaurant one day and enjoyed the attention of six waiters and waitresses who had no other customers to serve: the dining facility had opened a few days previously, but apparently no one in the city had as yet heard the news. Consulting the menu brought no results, since the waiter most proficient in English informed us that "the lunch" was prepared and awaited only our nod of the head for it to be served. We persisted, however, in communicating our desire not for a six-course meal but rather a light repas of salads and olives and bread. Persistence pays if one is polite enough, and the serving team finally allowed as how the kitchen could indeed prepare the meal we by now ravenously wanted.

The Grande Corniche along the harbor is jammed with strollers in the evening hours, with vendors of various items such as roasted corn cobs, nuts, ice cream, popcorn, and the like, serving them. Egyptians, like Greeks, eat supper after 10 pm so they require a bit of sustenance during their crepuscular constitutionals. Being neither Greek nor Egyptian, *after* our dinner Lynn-Marie and I would stroll along with the crowd and sit on the breakwater at the foot of the square by the Cecil to enjoy the cooler temperature and watch the perambulating crowd, some of whom kept an eye on us, no doubt wondering what these two middle aged Europeans were doing there at that hour. We spent a half hour one night talking to five young men, teachers from Cairo on a week's holiday at the sea. They were interested in what had brought us to the city, but when we mentioned Durrell their blank faces spoke reams about the local patriotism of the Egyptian education system. Alexandria has become a popular resort for Cairenes who seek to escape from the noise, heat and dirt of their city to the noise, heat and dirt of the northern city, expecting with some justification that the sea breeze will make all the difference.

Zaad (or Saad) Zaghloul (1860-1927) was a nationalist politician who helped Egypt along the road to independence from the British, though he did not live to see the day himself. The Stalinist statue you see in the middle of the square is a representation of this gentleman, upon which children climb and birds move whatever birds have for bowels.

Cavafy's third floor apartment for the last 25 years of his life at 4 Sharia Sharm el-Sheikh street (formerly rue Lepsius) is now a museum of sorts supported by the Greek government, the Egyptian government not being interested in a queer Greek who never learned to speak Arabic properly and who diddled young Arab men (at least the Egyptians assume they were young Arab men, whilst they may in fact have been young Greek godlets, since Cavafy couldn't speak Arabic; but perhaps he didn't need to converse at length with the boys in any case....). C. P. Cavafy is one of the great poets of the 20th century,[21] whose work

---

[21] In English his work is most readily available in the *Collected Poems* (edited by George Savidis, translated by Edmund Keeley and Philip Sherrard) published by Princeton University Press in paperback. But there are now many different translations in and out of print such as those by Rae Dalven (1961), John Mavrogordato (1951) Theoharis Constantine Theoharis (2001) and in 2004 a privately printed edition of yet another translation appeared in Athens. Furthermore, Anthony Hirst of Queen's University Belfast is preparing a critical edition of Cavafy's published works. One might also profitably look into Keeley's *Cavafy's Alexandria*, also from Princeton (1976, rev. 1996). There is as yet no good biography of the poet, but there is of his later compatriot and, until the publication of *Bitter Lemons* (1957), a friend of Lawrence Durrell: see Roderick Beaton, *George Seferis: Waiting for the Angel. A Biography* (New Haven CT, 2003). Robert Liddell (*Cavafy: A Biography* [New York, 1974]) attempted not very

every literate person should know. The Greek curator at the Cavafy Museum spoke to us in a happily confusing mélange of French and English, and gave us the wrong directions to Cavafy's tomb (tombs are very big in Egyptian culture, *vide* the Valleys of the Kings and Queens in Luxor, etc.) and we ended up at the old Jewish cemetery next to the Shallalat Gardens, interesting to be sure, but not Cavafy.[22]

Regarding the location of his apartment, the poet famously (is alleged to have) said, while standing on his tiny balcony, "Where could I live better? Below, the brothel caters for the flesh. And there is the church that forgives sin. And there is the hospital where we die." The cellar of the building is now a carpenter's shop; the Greek Orthodox Church of St. Saba is closed "for renovation," but is unlikely ever to open again; and the Greek hospital has long since ceased to exist. Cavafy did in fact die of cancer in it.

---

successfully a life of the poet, but I recall the book as being very *annoying*.

[22]Today one could almost claim that Cavafy is, like the Scarlet Pimpernel, not in heaven and not in hell, but everywhere: in his book, *Inside Hitler's Greece. The Experience of Occupation 1941-44* (1993), Mark Mazower notes that as the Germans converged on Athens in April 1941, the writer G. Theotokas wrote down lines from Cavafy's poem "Waiting for the Barbarians" (1904) in his diary ("What are we waiting for, gathered in the market place?/The barbarians will come today/,,,"). Theotokas, as Mazower points out, neglects the point of the Cavafy poem since, in the end, the barbarians do not come, and the waiting citizens wonder what they will do without them! Greeks in 1941 would much rather the barbarians of that day not have showed up.

The Cavafy Museum is one of the points of interest to Durrellians for whom the conference organizers arranged a walking tour.[23] Since we had already visited most of these places, we did not go along on the tour. Indeed, the major site we did not visit is the endangered villa in which Durrell lived during his years in the city, but this seemingly odd behavior is not unusual for us: we have been in Paris dozens of times and I've written a book about the city, but we've never explored the old Bibliothèque Nationale; we lived in a village outside Avignon for a year and have visited the city of the popes every year since 1985, but we've never danced on or under the pont d'Avignon ... some things one saves for the future, whenever that might be. In Alexandria we did, however, listen to the lecture given by a young architect of the city about the efforts being made by him and several others to save not only the Durrell villa, in addition to other "European" buildings from the insatiable molochian greed of the devil-opers. The chances of these efforts achieving success are not great.

---

[23]In 1977, Peter Adams made a film following Lawrence Durrell around his old haunts in Egypt, *Spirit of Place: Egypt* (BBC), one shot in which shows Durrell sitting at Cavafy's desk writing a postal card to Henry Miller. There is no indication that Durrell even visited the apartment during his enforced stay in the city during the war. The text of the card is reproduced in Ian S. MacNiven (ed.), *The Durrell-Miller Letters, 1935-80* (London, 1988), 488.

A list of the places visited on our tours contains the centuries of Alexandrine history, from the founding of the city in 331 BCE down the echoing corridors of time until Egyptian independence: the Graeco-Roman Museum, Pompey's Pillar, the Roman theater and baths at Kom el Dikka near the railroad station, the Kom el-Shogafa catacombs, the Montazah Palace and Gardens, the café-restaurant-patisseries Pastroudis (a favorite of Cavafy and the characters in *The Quartet,* whose kitchen prepared our bus tour lunch boxes), the Trianon (in the Metropole Hotel building), the Athineos ... One does notice a curious absence of things related to the period of the Arab (642-1517 CE) and Ottoman Turk (1517-1798) occupations. Ibn Tulun, who ruled 868 to 884 CE, declared Egypt to be independent of the so-called Arab Empire and restored the site of the Pharos Lighthouse, one of the Seven Wonders of the World, and the Mameluke sultan, Qayt Bey constructed a fort on the Pharos site, called today with some justification Fort Qayt Bey. Here the Durrellians and other inhabitants of the city gathered one night for an hour of "folkloric" singing and dancing, an entertainment that began hours late due to a traffic accident involving the entertainers' bus. Once one moved away from the loudspeakers blasting the electrified music at painful levels, one found the entertainment quite entertaining. Not far from the Fort along the

Corniche is the Tikka Fish Market restaurant, the second floor of which overlooks the Eastern Harbor, where the conference participants lunched one day. The food here was very good. We all drank bottled mineral water, a highly recommended habit to form when in the Middle East.

Our machine-gun toting guards escorted us to the site of one of the important World War Two battlefields, appropriately enough since the war plays such a large role in *The Quartet*. The El Alamein military museum and cemeteries may be of no interest to most people, which is unfortunate because once one is there it is fascinating to follow the crazy-quilt pattern of the early November 1942 battle on the museum's broad table relief model, complete with differently colored tiny light bulbs, which aid in comprehending the first real Allied military victory against the Axis (followed by the American landings in northwest Africa a few days later). The Egyptians who created and maintain the museum can be forgiven for inflating the importance of the Egyptian army's contribution to that victory. The typology of the military cemeteries reflects the national origins of those buried in the three we saw: the British is subdued and spread over a vast low beige landscape, the German is a dark bulky fortress of stone exuding power and authority reminiscent of a Crusader fortress, the Italian is tall and tries to be elegant.

On the return trip we stopped at a seaside resort, the name of which I do not recall, to swim and relax with drinks and olives. The security staff did not swim. Nor did I, because I never learned the trick of it. Instead, I joined a bantering conversation with several other Durrellians who, for one reason or another, did not find the Mediterranean waters sufficiently enticing to enter into them. We drank Stella beer, local not export, the quality of which often changed dramatically with each new bottle. In fact, we drank quite a bit of Stella local because the Egyptian wine, how shall one phrase it, does not quite rise to a level above the barely drinkable. Cooling white wine does not seem to be a custom most Egyptians have taken to with any consistency or enthusiasm. Another reason for drinking Stella local is the large portions of peanuts simply *encrusted*, mon, with saliva-provoking chunks of *salt,* which I never use in cooking, of course. The peanuts, I must admit, I consumed with passion and delight, and drank lots of Stella local.

And speaking of delight and Stella local, the Egyptian conference co-chairperson, Soad Hussein Sobhy, and her pediatrician husband, Galal Aref, invited the Durrellians to their summer cabin on the grounds of the old Montazah Palace Gardens close to the beach there, where one can swim in relative peace and cleanliness. Some years ago, someone or some organization, possibly the government, erected a series of small two-story townhouse-like structures, which can be rented by the year and here we spent a joyful afternoon and evening. Our hosts provided plenty to eat (grilled meats, salads, olives, fresh vegetables and fruits) and plenty of bottled mineral water and Stella local. Many guests actually even swam in the warmish Mediterranean. Everyone appreciated this gesture of hospitality and friendliness, qualities shared by Soad and Galal with many of their fellow Egyptians. Though not necessarily by Egyptian taxi drivers, one of whose main missions in life is, by carefully controlled experiments, to determine how quickly they can frighten their European customers into a state of catatonic shock.[24]

The final night of the conference proved to be the wildest, if one understands "wild" in the context of a group of mostly aging academics. The Alexandrian organizers rented a hall in the new branch of Pastroudis out on the Corniche to the East, heading in the direction of Montazah. A buffet dinner and entertainment accompanied the wine, beer and mineral water. (This time Lynn-Marie and I drank the wine, but not very much of it.) The entertainment consisted of a small

---

[24]In fairness, it must be said that the drivers do possess a talent for graceful maneuvering in dense traffic at unbelievably high speeds that would make their Parisian and New York colleagues drool with envy. The grace does not always guarantee an undamaged trip, as the dents and cracks in most taxi cab bodies attest.

electrified band, a "famous Egyptian crooner," our own sedate ballroom style dancing, and, as a finale, a wowser of a belly dancer, reputed to be one of the best in the region, who knocked everyone out, especially those she tempted on to the dance floor to help her out!

Can anyone imagine an academic conference such as this one in North America? Or on the European mainland? I've been to many conferences on both continents, but nothing like this one. Ouf![25]

Luxor

The day following the conference, exhausted but still stimulated,[26] the two of us left for Luxor, but not in the manner we had planned, which was to fly to Cairo, change planes and fly to Luxor. As

---

[25]There is no mention here of the papers presented at the conference sessions because such a discussion would burst the integument of this informal travel essay and, frankly, would bore readers not interested in Durrell's works and related subjects.

[26]The varied stimulation caused by the conference, the city, and reacquainting oneself with *The Quartet* worked in curious ways on all of us, no doubt. For myself, I came back from Alexandria with a good dozen pages of notes for a trilogy of novels about Berlin in the 20th century, which I began in 1981 and had not touched since 1984. *This*, I suggest, is one of the conference's achievements. The ILDS conferences on the Greek islands of Corfu (2000) and Rhodes (2004) had similar effects on this work. That the series is not yet finished is not the fault of the gatherings. The Corfu conference is, however, at least indirectly responsible for the creation of the Durrell School of Corfu by its academic director, Richard Pine, but that story is the subject of separate essay, printed elsewhere in this volume.

fate would have it, the Arab summit met the same week in Cairo to determine the Arabs' response to the election of the conservative hardliner, Binjamin Netanyahu as Israeli prime minister. For some reason this caused the Egyptian security directorate to cancel all flights between Alexandria and Cairo. Consequently, the official Egyptian travel agency, through which we had booked the flight, the hotel in Luxor, and the guide and transportation there, sent us an old, but air conditioned Mercedes with manic but personable driver to move us from the Cecil to the Cairo airport, some 150 kilometers to the south down a dusty potholed road through the desert. All went reasonably well, but from the outskirts of Cairo to the airport I closed my eyes and breathed slowly and deeply from the lower abdomen.

At Luxor we stayed in the Old Winter Palace Hotel, part of the Sofitel chain, to which the Cecil also now belongs, and not to be confused with the recently constructed New Winter Palace, a massive box with no redeeming qualities; the locals, none of whom could possibly afford either one, in order to distinguish between them, refer with faux innocent charm to the original simply as "The Old." In context this is truly a palace. Built by the British in 1887, it exudes imperial luxury: vast gardens, vast hallways, a vast swimming pool with a bar in the middle! I actually dipped into the pool my veryownself twice in the early evening hours before changing for dinner.

The hotel boasts a French restaurant named "1789," with a menu of familiar dishes, which may have tasted as delicious as those at a three-star Parisian eatery, but we preferred to eat at the local restaurants for reasons of principle and financial considerations. The Royal Bar almost lives up to its name (a billiard table room is attached to it, whose walls are lined with book cases filled with English, French, German, Italian and some Arabic language books on Egypt and other subjects, none of which seems to have been published after 1932). We sat happily there listening to a rather mechanical piano player pound away at the old upright whilst we drank Stella local and ate the salted nuts.

The guest rooms facing the Nile are also vast, but we stayed in a less vast accommodation facing the gardens in the back, which is fine with me since it also faced the East which means it did not suffer from the afternoon sun, which can be very uncomfortable when one wishes to take a nap, even in air conditioned rooms, which of course the Old Winter Palace offers. If one had Nabokov's residential inclinations and his late in life income, one could actually live in that luxury.

I find tombs, temples and monuments of interest during the time I am with them, but for some reason my interest wanes considerably after

I've left them. Consequently, I retain only fragments of images embedded in my memory from the three days we spent in Luxor. This has less to do with the attractions of the place than with my own inability to retain a clear recall of many of my experiences, a characteristic of some advantage at times, but not when composing a travel memoir. Nonetheless here is what is remembered.

-- The heat: 110 degrees Fahrenheit in the shade; dry heat, to be sure, and at this level if one does not drink several liters of water a day, one becomes dehydrated and very sick. We carried a liter each whenever we left the hotel and always returned with empty bottles.

-- The taxi and calèche drivers begin their importuning a block before you reach them. It requires an inordinate amount of patience and politeness to get along walking in the streets. "No thanks," with the appropriate negative gestures, must be repeated over and over as one strolls about. We did not, however, experience many beggars of any age.

-- The massive dimensions of the Mortuary Temple of Hatshepsut at Deir el-Bahri on the West Bank, toward which one walks forever on a broad promenade in the blazing sunlight (wearing one's absolutely required head covering), are overwhelming.

-- The small dimensions of Tutankhamun's tomb; its importance lies not in its size but in the fact that Howard Carter and his colleagues discovered it intact. Only the sarcophagus containing the king's mummy remains in the tomb. Removing the contents took Carter's crew ten years; the artifacts are now in the Cairo museum.[27]

-- A prolonged taxi ride from one temple to the next (Karnak to Luxor), the prolongation of which was caused by the police shutting down the main street along the Nile because of a visit by the Egyptian defense minister and his entourage (checking the tombs for possible military use no doubt).

-- The dramatically effective sound and light show at the Karnak Temples unfortunately went on 30 minutes too long.

-- Walking among the colossal Karnack monuments, impressive despite the gaggles of tourists in one's way, blocking one's view and clogging one's ears with their babbling banalities, is an experience that remains with one, despite the disclaimer made above. Needless to say, we do not consider ourselves tourists, but rather literate (and quiet) visitors to the past.

-- The bookstore down the Corniche from the Old Winter Palace sells newspapers only five days

---

[27]By all means read the profusely illustrated *The Discovery of the Tomb of Tutankhamen* by Howard Carter and A.C. Mace (1923), kept in print by the good people at Dover Publications.

old, but this is balanced by the fact that one can purchase readable copies of Mahfouz's works and Krimis in various languages with faded covers and sand in the pages.

-- The pleasant, well-watered dinner with some friends and colleagues from the conference on their way further south to Aswan and beyond neatly broke the sense of being alone in a strange world.

-- The utter, ear-crushing chaos at the airport and the calm but persistent actions of the travel agency's representative who took care of us in Luxor made us grateful for having booked in advance.

We left several things unvisited so we will have something new to do should we return to Luxor (the Luxor Museum; the souk; the restaurant on the Lotus, a boat which has "dinner cruises with oriental show"; the University of Chicago Oriental Institute's library...), in addition to Aswan and beyond.

We flew to Cairo and then on to Alexandria, the summit having concluded its business thus allowing Egypt Air to resume its regularly scheduled flights, arriving at the Cecil in the early afternoon, at which point I collapsed into a nap. Many stores remain open until late at night, but close midday, so enabling us later that evening to visit a shop or two in the gold jewelry district, where a friendly but persistent hustler simply refused to believe that we could get along for the rest of our stay in the city without his "guaranteed cheap" assistance. We finally convinced him. We ate dinner that last night in Egypt at a small, un-air conditioned restaurant called Chez Denis on a narrow street running away from the harbor, where we had the best meal in the country: grilled shrimps, various salads, olives, and a grilled whole fish of unknown provenance for each of us. The seafood we had picked out ourselves in the kitchen, because as in Greece, one chooses one's own fish from the catch of the day. Mineral water, of course, and a bottle of relatively cooled white wine, which the cook's assistant had to go out and buy in a wine store. We ate at nine, no other customers entered the place. Egyptians, like the Greeks, eat very late.

Very early the next morning we enjoyed a thrilling taxi roller coaster to the airport in order to fly to Athens. The cab driver allowed himself to be satisfied with double the fare rather than triple, which we refused, smiling politely all the while.

Athens

After a brief and pleasant Olympic Airlines flight over the ostentatiously blue Mediterranean and numerous islands of various sizes, we landed in the somewhat less intense heat and sunshine of Athens, a city of vast contrasts, which perhaps can be summed up this way: the carcinogenic pollution from the internal combustion gasoline-powered engine is eating away the austere beauty of the ancient Acropolis.

Aphrodite waited for us as we emerged from the customs area. The previous ten years since we had last seen her had made no inroads on her loveliness; nor had the lengthy absence dimmed the warmth with which we greeted each other. The years slipped away ... Without pause, and with an enviable talent for navigating the treacherous shoals of Athenian traffic, she drove us to the small (but air conditioned!) apartment on the fifth and top floor of a building across the street from her large family apartment. With its long balcony and magnificent view of the city and the surrounding hills, including Lycabettus with its perched open-air theater, this would be our headquarters during our stay in Athens, a welcome jewel in the crown of our trip!

Public advertising in Europe is far sexier (or, to a feminist, no doubt "sexist") than the almost-pornography one sees in the USA. Indeed, the barely covered but well-rounded bottom sticking out from under a beach umbrella would hardly inform the onlooker that the advertisement flogs a brand of washing powder, the name of which appeared in small letters at the bottom of the billboard. Nor did the photograph of the erotically posed woman in color, collaged over an old black and white image of men sitting and standing around a small but appropriately quaint village square, appear to have any relationship to the brand of cigarettes thusly advertised. And what about that photograph of that young woman in that black leather thong bikini with her legs...? These things stand out when one views them as foreground to the Acropolis.

The National Art Gallery is an interesting building, air conditioned, but the temporary exhibition during our visit unfortunately consisted of crap the Whitney Museum in New York calls "contemporary art." The garden contains some attractive sculpture, some pieces of which get watered along with the grass, and a Magritte sculpture of a seated figure sits alone on an unapproachable balcony, a birdcage for a torso. The permanent exhibition of 19th and 20th century Greek art is worth the price of admission; it is not often that those of us who live outside Greece have the opportunity to see the influence of the great European and American art movements on Greek artists.

The Gennadis Library is a peaceful and cool haven amidst the heat and din of Athens. We saw there a small exhibition of original watercolors with the Greek war for independence (1821-1832) as the subject made in the 19th century for engraving reproductions. It would be pleasant to conduct research here.

We walked more than most Athenians, but only because we couldn't bear the thought of un-air conditioned taxis driven by cigarette puffing dragomen, unless absolutely necessary, and we never did get the hang of the bus system. Frankly, what one remembers most is not the Acropolis, the old Jewish Museum (though this is fascinating and full of history), or the other major tourist sites, but rather sitting in a marina restaurant outside the city along the shore toward the old airport eating the myriad first courses and giant fresh shrimp with wonderfully dry white wine and the inevitable (for the two of us: a glass of water with each glass of wine saves wear and tear on the head next day) mineral water, and the bubbling company of Aphrodite and her husband, Yannis.

One night around 9:30 they took us to the terrace of a garden restaurant in the middle of the city and we wondered how this deserted place could stay in business: by midnight you could not find a seat unless you might be a well-known politician or television news reader, several of whom did arrive "late," but found a table. The restaurant is located on the edge of a park next to a large villa on the edge of the park, now called Liberation House, because several of the many opponents of the so-called "colonels'" regime who ended up there, were tortured by the secret police, survived their horrible experiences and were liberated by the restoration of democracy not too long ago.[28] The park is called Pedion tou Areos (literally "field of mars") to commemorate the heroes of the liberation struggle against the Turks early in the 19th century.

We associate food with many of our friends and these are among them. Down the hill from their apartment, no more than 50 meters away, there is a restaurant so secluded one would never find it alone except by the purest of accidents. We are greeted by the waiters and the owner with warmth and noise, and seated on a terrace only as wide as the table, where we non-Greek-speaking types listened to the lengthy Greek conversation relating to the meal and how it would be served. We understood only the word "evcharisto" (thank you), but the meal that followed met every standard for a rather spontaneous occasion. A seemingly unending flow of small plates filled with sharply tasty delicacies began to appear as soon as the owner poured the cool, clear wine from his own vineyard into our glasses. These little miracles of flavor would have sufficed for me, but the second course followed: fish, grilled lamb, pasta ... no

---

[28]In April 1967, a group of Greek army colonels executed a coup d'état against the government and inaugurated an era of right-wing terror that might truthfully be called fascist. The regime fell apart and democracy was restored in 1974. To gain an inkling of what this vicious military dictatorship was like, see the taut and passionate thriller, *Z* by Costa-Gavras (1969) with a cast that could not be better, including Yves Montand, Jean-Louis Trintignant, Charles Denner, Jacques Perrin and the great Irene Papas, who never utters a word.

dessert, please. There are times when eating a meal is a pleasantly exhausting process.

It is a tradition with us to look for bookstores wherever we travel to see if there are books of interest not published in the United States and to feed my fetish of collecting only British editions of a number of British writers. There are several such shops in the city, all around Syntagma Square, but one can buy newspapers from northern European countries in kiosks around Kolonaki Square through which we walked several times on our way elsewhere, and where we had small lunches (given the dinners, lunches had to be minuscule) on the terrace of one of the bistros along one side of the square. Unfortunately, the Greeks have not escaped the toxic infection of the noise plague in its worst form: so-called music in eating establishments. We've left restaurants and terraced bistros in several countries, including out own, because of this misguided effort at increasing the volume of clientele. However, if you can find a taverna with terrace on a busy corner in the Plaka, you may safely rest there for lunch. The music is at least played softly and includes Yves Montand. At any rate this has been our experience.

Yannis arranged a taxi to the port of Piraeus for us to find the *Rodos*, the "ferry," as the Greeks call it (I think of it as a fully-fledged ship), which would bear us through the waters of the Aegean to the island of Rhodes. We asked Yannis to arrange the taxi, driven by a friend of his, because the government had announced that no private motor vehicles would be allowed in the city center during the day: the temperature and the pollution levels would be too high. Monuments that withstood centuries of wind, sun and rains, are crumbling into dust under the relentless onslaught of the gasoline-powered motor vehicle. The effect on humans appears to be irrelevant, never mind, but the tourists expect to see *something* left of the Acropolis so it must be protected, n'est-ce pas?

Those who expect Piraeus to appear as the representations of it appear in *Zorba the Greek* and *Never on Sunday* will be sorely disappointed to find it a relatively characterless business-like harbor, organized to be as efficient and as profitable as possible. There is, however, no substitute for sailing to the islands, even on a motor-powered boat. Flying is boring and swift. Sailing or steaming, ah well ... And where else can one vicariously experience the sweet-sad parting of young lovers, the girl forlornly on the dock looking up and waving, the boy on the third deck leaning over the rail waving back intently, willing the boat to leave and so break the spell that pained them both. The boat sailed 20 minutes later; the girl remained on the dock until the end.

Rhodes

At approximately 18.30 hours on board the *Rodos,* on the overnight run from Piraeus to Rhodes, a group of Gypsies have planted themselves underneath the stairs on the interior of the second deck with a sort of Bunsen burner or hibachi over which they are cooking something to eat. Coming upon the scene, the Greek ship's officer is flabbergasted into speechlessness, eyes bulging in disbelief. He sternly admonishes them that this behavior is against the law and dangerous to the ship and its passenger, something of course the Gypsies know without hearing it from him. They laugh and give each other the bent eye. Chuckling, they continued to cook and eat what, by Mediterranean standards, is an early evening meal.

Earlier several of the Gypsies had conducted a vociferously loud and loudly dramatic altercation with the ship's purser about some issue of contention having apparently to do with tickets or the lack thereof, during which an older woman, shouting Greek at the top of her deep voice, grabbed a youngster of five or six and held him up to the purser clearly yelling something about this poor innocent child having to sleep out on the deck all night in the cold damp and pneumonia-making sea air. Because it appeared that the argument would continue for the foreseeable future, I continued on my way to the ship's saloon, thinking about the many passengers who had paid for tickets to sleep on the deck and the fact that thirty minutes earlier a large group of Gypsies, to whom these bellowing individuals belonged, had transported a mass of pillows, quilts and sleeping bags from one deck to another, clearly ready to bed down on the deck for the night. There are phenomena about which one can only shake one's head and pass on.

Now, the ship's officer, finally finding his full-authority voice, begins to remonstrate with increasing volume, and seeing that this situation could also proceed indefinitely I continued on my way to the men's room. Some time later, we noticed that the ship's officer must have been successful because the area under the stairs no longer contained cooking utensils or people to use them. We did not see the Gypsies again and wondered if they lived on Rhodes or were just visiting.

Coming into a harbor is always an exciting phenomenon, and entering Rhodes Town port is no exception. Shortly after sunrise we first viewed the island and an hour later the boat rounded the point and we began to maneuver to enter the harbor proper, small with its buildings clumped close together, a working harbor. The tourist harbor with tour boats and cafés is a kilometer or so away. One walks quite a distance to reach the line of taxis, but things move swiftly from then on, and, if one stays where we stayed, the drive takes one down the east coast past an all too lengthy list of large clunky resort hotels with names like "Paradise" and "Ulysses." When an overbearing cement and glass resort hotel desecrating a seashore is called "Paradise," you know you are in the wrong place.

We settled quickly into our own demi-pension clunker, the Hotel Kalypso, which in no way resembles the Old Winter Palace except for the (much smaller) swimming pool. This modern resort caters to large white and red-striped German, Swiss and English (with a modicum of Italian) tour groups and the staff speaks a sufficient amount of all European languages to attend to the needs of their often badly behaved clientele. In the Old Winter Palace one never saw bare-breasted women of any age, much less of all ages, at the swimming pool. Not that one has anything against this manner of achieving skin cancer in principle, but some people, myself included, are simply not constructed, at least not any longer, to be viewed in an undressed state with any pleasure. Oh, well ... The bar served a decent single malt scotch whisky and a fine draft pilsner to go with the salted nuts, the food remained consistently edible, the public bus appeared on schedule, and our waitress became quite fond of us, and served us a fine Rhodian white wine.

After checking in and complaining about the malfunctioning air conditioner (to little avail, but the nights are cool), we took the number 20 bus into Rhodes Town to walk around, see the museums, and eat lunch on a second floor roof restaurant across a small lane from the abandoned and dilapidated mosque of Suleiman the Magnificent on Socrates Street in the old city. This part of the town is within the original city walls and is devoted to museums in praise of the greatness of Rhodes' past and to tourists, which support the island's present. Except for the museums (one of which contains the two marine Venus statues), several churches, Ministry of Culture offices, the entire old town is jammed with restaurants, tavernas and stores selling the usual tourist kitsch. It is a horror. Indeed, the entire coast of the island, wherever humans have put their architectural mark, is a nightmare of high-rise hotels and attendant businesses. The new town is also a shopping mall, but often without the scads of tourboat gushings and some of the architecture is of interest. But walk around the back and side streets of the old town and you'll come upon sudden archeological digs in someone's backyard, in which scrawny cats roam at will, searching for that ancient heavenly cat fix. You cannot always escape the tourists, but sometimes you can ignore them.

The Villa Cleobolus, actually a tiny building with two small rooms and a toilet, where Durrell lived with his second wife, Eve Cohen, during their sojourn on Rhodes in 1945-47 and about which he writes with such affection in *Reflections on a Marine Venus*, a book that rewards many readings, is located near the Mourad Reis Mosque. It sits on the edge of a garden which contains the old Turkish cemetery a stone's throw from a large pinkish building, which used to be the elegant Albergo della Rosa, where Eve lived and where Durrell and his colleagues were put up by the military authorities immediately upon their arrival on the island in 1945. It is now deserted, as is the Villa Cleobolus,[29] which, however, boasts a plaque on its street façade stating in Greek and English

In this house lived the
philhellene and friend
of Rhodes
poet and novelist
Lawrence G. Durrell
From 20-5-1945 to 10-4-1947

On the west coast of the island, the Kameiros ancient city dig is also described in *Reflections*, but

---

[29]Since 1996 when this essay was written, the Albergo has become a glitzy gambling den called the Rhodes Casino and the villa is now contains the office of the International Writers and Translators Center of Rhodes. The plaque remains in place. (2004)

rather fancifully I think, though we were not there in the evening, nor did we picnic on its ruined walls. We did eat at the Blue Sea Taverna, which is on the beach at the foot of the hill upon which the ruins of Kameiros sit, and is a pleasant exception to the "jam in as many tourists as possible" rule, so avidly followed on Rhodes. The small cuddly two-month-old German shepherd doggy chewed happily on my toes and sandals whilst we drank local wine and ate an assortment of local dishes (taramasalata, cucumbers with onions, green peppers and tomatoes, tzazikis [thick yogurt mixed with dill and onion], souflaki [warm pieces of lamb in an otherwise cool salad]) ... The Ilios white wine of Rhodes is reasonably priced, rather bland, but very drinkable and fine for a late hot-weather lunch on the shore.

This description of our Rhodes sojourn would be incomplete without mention of the Alexis restaurant in the middle of the old part of Rhodes Town. We arrived after 8 pm to discover the place devoid of customers, as usual, but this time we did not worry about the poor owner going bankrupt, by ten o'clock, we by now knew, empty bellies would fill every chair. Alexis only serves seafood, a fact specifically noted in its advertisements and stated on the telephone when one makes reservations. After choosing your own fish, you return to the table to nibble on olives and feta cheese as the young waiter cautiously pours chilled white Ilios into a clean wine glass (no water glasses here!). If I say that we recommend the place, you can be assured we thoroughly enjoyed the food.[30]

And, what is more unusual, the other customers did not disturb our enjoyment. Indeed, we watched with fascination as a group of four sat at a nearby table and began to study the menu, that is the older bearded bald gentleman, resembling in appearance and distracted behavior nothing so much as the absent-minded professor not too far from retirement, and the very much younger woman with long dark hair and what is often described as "olive skin," studied the menu. The two girls, we guessed their ages to be around eight and ten, presumably their daughters, but who knows, sought no advice from the menu (which had both Greek and English listings), but demanded soft-drinks and pommes frites, which they indeed obtained. Papa, if indeed it was papa, ordered a mountain of mussels, which he consumed with enthusiasm, but with which he drank, I gag to even write it down, *orange juice!* They all thoroughly enjoyed themselves, the kids did not make much racket. Unfortunately the photographs I took, allegedly of Lynn-Marie but with the family in the background, do not show

---

[30]Again, keep in mind when this was originally written. On a visit to the island in the summer of 2004 (another Durrell Society conference with a still lovely Eve Cohen Durrell in attendance!), the restaurant was still serving, but we did not eat there and it may no longer limit its menu to seafood.

any details of the four happy people, the camera is too primitive.

Speaking of wine, one should not fail to visit the Emery vineyard just outside Embonas, some kilometers inland from the west coast. It is not easy to find, but well worth the effort. When we asked which firm distributes the wine in the USA, a guffaw and smiles greeted the question. The volume of production is so limited that the winery distributes this elixir only to Rhodes itself, near-by islands, and very few bottles to certain restaurants in Athens. Tant pis pour nous. It is delicious and dances on your tongue.

There are other sites worth visiting on the island, for example the valley of the butterflies, where only the group of Italian tourists refused to abide by the injunction to be as quiet as possible so as not to disturb the beautiful creatures, and the perched fortress at Kastelos with its exhausting climb and vast panoramic view, but all this talk of wine has exhausted me and made me thirsty.

As is always the case when one thinks back on a trip many other people and things seen come to mind, but this missive is long enough and at this point can be brought to a close, before everyone's patience is at an end, including the author's.

With best regards, I remain

Blessing the Sea at
Les Saintes-Maries-de-la-mer

DURING SATURDAY NIGHT VESPERS the painted wooden figure of the two Marys in their boat had been lowered from the ceiling of the church to rest before the altar where the pilgrims crowded around to touch it. In the early chill of Sunday morning a young man dressed in thick brown corduroy trousers and a blue pullover drove the McCormick tractor from the garage to the beach. In the sea mist he hooked a small wooden boat to the tractor and towed it across the sand to a point near the water. Then he drove the tractor back to the road along the beach and, shivering only slightly, patiently waited.

Because it was the end of October and filled with gray rain the day did not attract the usual numbers of tourists to the former fishing village on the edge of the Camargue, but they still outnumbered by far the worshippers. Some had come in automobiles the night before to stay at one of the bleached, summer-worn hotels that remained open, but most of them arrived in oversized tourist buses that morning.

In the square before the Romanesque church the working cowboys of the Camargue, called gardiens, and the local families who could not find a place inside waited among the tourists with flashing cameras and a few gypsies who pinned small plastic medals on the tourists' jackets for a few francs. Behind the ornate wooden doors the priests and acolytes served the mass and preached the traditional sermon.

When the priests threw open the doors and emerged from the church, the gardiens formed two rows to lead the procession, urging their horses against the tourists who were pushing and shoving to get a better view. Then the crude blue boat and carved figures appeared and the air filled with the snapping of cameras and whining voices. Ignoring the disturbance, the procession moved with some dignity through the narrow mist-shrouded white streets toward the beach and the Mediterranean waters.

As they approached the sand, the clerics chanted even louder to be heard over the noise of the surf. They crossed the beach slowly toward the waiting boat. The gardiens rode past the boat and spurred their stocky horses a few meters into the sea where they turned to face the shore. Three priests climbed awkwardly into the boat and held on to the thin mast; between them and the gardiens the relics of the saints rested on the shoulders of six men chosen from the villagers. The priest representing the bishop raised his battery-powered bullhorn and chanted a few phrases in Provençal to the sea. Cameras snapped in the cold damp air. Four young men staggered on to the beach smoking cigarettes and passing a bottle of red wine back and forth talking in loud voices.

The priests climbed out of the boat and the gardiens rode out of the surf on to the beach. Accompanied by the faithful, the procession headed back to the church just a little faster than it had marched to the sea. The tourists wandered off to find lunch before departing in their huge buses. Soon the beach was empty except for the young worker and the tractor dragging the small wooden boat across the sand through the empty cigarette packets and plastic wine bottles.

(Tavel, 1983)

The Narrative of a Less Than Sentimental Journey to France and Greece in May and June in the Year of Our Blessed If Difficult to Locate Virgins 2002

THE HOUSE WE RENTED site-unseen, except for a picture on the rental agency's web site in Villeneuve-lès-Avignon, directly across the Rhône river from the old City of the Popes, turned out to be a gem, to which we'd like to return each summer for several months (after one of my books becomes a bestseller and I get a monster advance for the next). Originally the two-story house served as the residence of the gardener for the chateau grounds; it contains a patio, living and dining rooms, kitchen, two bedrooms, a work room, and two toilets that more or less work regularly (the smell of drains, while not constant, is a presence, but this is a small price to pay for the advantages of the place), and sits in a fairly large garden filled with cherry trees, the fruit of which we ate every day courtesy of our landlady, who teaches medieval French literature at the university, which lent our conversations a slightly scholarly air. Since we lived in the early 1980s for a year in the neighboring village of Tavel, famous as the producer of the best rosé wine in the world,

122

we have returned for briefer visits with some regularity to see friends and experience anew the environs where we spent an extraordinarily happy period of our lives.

Food and drink have become one of the major standards by which we measure the success of a trip or sojourn away from home. Negative eating experiences can wreak havoc with travel and indelibly stain the memory. Thus we were pleased when our friend in L'isle-sur-la-Sorgue, Gustav Falk, took us to a marvelously friendly and architecturally fascinating restaurant called Le Prévoté in a former cloister over a narrow canal in the middle of the old town. One enters through a massive wood door and walks over a short glass bridge spanning the canal, then into a series of spaces and alcoves that appear to be carved out of solid beige stone and supported by thick wood beams. Sounds are muted by some invisible but welcome baffle system. The tables and chairs are made of heavy wood and covered with brightly colored Provençal cloths. The menu is deliberately limited and all the items on it are fresh and locally produced. The wine also comes from the local terroir, and while the prices are not bargain basement by any means, the food and ambience are so terrific, one pays gladly. There is usually a daily fixed menu for a reasonable price. The place deserves a Michelin star and we wrote to the Guide Rouge to strongly urge it receive one.

There are not many memorable meals in one's life, so those that qualify are well remembered, as is the restaurant called Le Brûleur de Loups in the Saintes-Maries-de-la-mer on the Mediterranean, where in 1982 I mistook the price of the lobster per gram for the price of the lobster per se, and paid heavily for the mistake. We have also eaten there later in the early 1990s during a visit from my brother Dean, a man who appreciates the same quality of food and drink that we do.

This year, on an unplanned impulse, we drove down for the day and ended up in the midst of a demented pack of motorcyclists, hundreds of them, roaring through the small streets, swarming around the boules courts in the main square, revving their engines in a cacophonous display of testosterone-driven machismo the likes of which we hadn't heard since the last biker week in Key West.

Happily they knocked off their stupidities for lunch (they are, after all, *French* bikers, despite their addiction to Harley-Davidsons and American blue jeans). We sat at an open corner window (the last table not reserved in advance!) and ate with relish, and in peace and quiet, grilled rougets, soupe au poisson with aïoli, and an ice cream tarte dessert, well watered with a fine dry white wine from the Languedoc. No blessing of the sea and guitar-strumming gypsies this time, that happens later in the month of May and again in October,[31] but we did note the distinct strains of the *M*A*S*H* theme as background music in the restaurant. We have no compunction about walking out of restaurants because of obnoxious music: the volume here, however, was soft enough to enchant with songs by Yves Montand, the inevitable Edith Piaf and the smoky voice of Serge Reggiani in addition to an occasional tune by Sinatra and Streisand (and, in the case of the *M*A*S*H* theme, amuse), but not disturb. Curious choice of tunes, we thought, for a restaurant overlooking the Mediterranean. We smiled and ordered another glass of wine. The sun caressed the town and the notion of having arrived in the promised land coursed gently through our minds.

Back in Avignon, we viewed Robert Altman's brilliant *Gosford Park* at the new Utopia movie theater, missing some of the poorly recorded vernacular English dialogue; the drift, however, was clear. The family-owned and-operated old Caleche restaurant in Villeneuve-lès-Avignon where so many years ago we ate the salads of warm tiny birds (quail, no doubt) and bibb lettuce drizzled with a warm vinaigrette closed for good so we could not repeat the experience, but we did dine twice at our second best Avignon Italian

---

[31] See "Blessing the Sea at Saintes-Maries-de-la-mer," elsewhere in this volume for a more detailed account of the autumn event as we witnessed it in 1982.

bistro called La Pizza, where we ate the eponymous dish and drank a lovely local red. (The first best was François' pizzeria on the Barthelasse island, which is now a "club privé" and no longer the locale of the best pizza in the world, which is now made by Lynn-Marie in our own kitchen.)[32]

Avignon intra muros hasn't changed much in the last ten years, and is still choked with tourists, but we know how to avoid most of them by now. We revisited the Musée Angladon stuck away off the rue de la Republique behind the Médiatèque Cedano (in an earlier life we called such things libraries) with its fine collection of modernist pieces by famous and not so famous French painters. And we found a new museum in Avignon called the Collection Lambert, filled with post-modern faux art and not worth a visit except for the building, which is vastly more interesting than its contents.

The village of Roussillon to the east of Avignon in the Vaucluse sits perched on a hill of ochre colored earth; it is a larger version of a "perched village" and served Laurence Wylie and his family as a home in the early 1950s, a sojourn that resulted in the classic sociological study, *Village in the Vaucluse*, first published in 1958 and subsequently in a third edition in 1976, wherein

---

[32] For additional details about François and his pizza, see "Gunsmoke and Provençal Sunday Pizza (A Cowboy Culinary, Euro-American Adventure)" elsewhere in this volume.

the village is called Peyrane for various reasons, although by the third edition Wylie gave the game away in the preface. Not that the pseudonym fooled the villagers who read the French edition and reacted variously to their portraits. The area has been a home to various artists and writers. Samuel Beckett lived there clandestinely during the war; Jean Lacoutre, the journalist whose biographies of de Gaulle and Malraux set the standard, lives in the former Wylie residence; and for decades the artist-ceramicist, Eugène Fidler lived and worked there with his wife Edith. We are fortunate enough to own several of his works in various media in addition to those by Edith and their daughter Natalie, who are also fine ceramicists. Their works hang in many private and public collections. Eugène died in 1990 at the age of 80; Edith and Natalie carry on the family tradition in the Roussillon studio. Eugène had a good command of English, one reason for which is the fact that Beckett taught him the rudiments of the language while they both hid out from the Vichy police and the Gestapo who wanted them for resistance activities. We have known the Fidlers since 1981 and never fail to visit them when we are resident in the Midi. And Edith never fails to serve an excellent multi-course lunch, well-watered (bien arrosé) with the product of the local vineyards.

One of the pleasures of spending time in France is watching certain programs on the television. When we lived in Tavel for a year two decades ago we bought a tiny black and white TV and were rather astonished one evening to see a bare-breasted young woman ironing a blouse, which she then put on and went about her business. The show was a comedy. Later we particularly enjoyed watching a young couple called Les Zaptualités, who traded snappy political and cultural one-liners with the show's host, Michel Drucker; while we didn't understand all of the repartee, the drift was clear enough. Alas, the Zapts are no longer on the air, and Drucker has a different show, but all his programs over the last 30 years have one thing in common: they resemble the late-night talk and performance shows so popular and longstanding in the USA.

On this trip on the television one night we saw a movie you'll never see on the TV in the USA: Henri Verneuil's 1966 "western" called *Cent mille dollars au soleil* with the young Jean-Paul Belmondo and the ever grand Lino Ventura, a sort of remake of Henri-Georges Clouzot's classic 1955 film, *Le salaire de la peur* (*Wages of Fear*), Belmondo and Ventura splitting the Yves Montand and Peter Van Eyck roles right down the Sahara middle (supposedly Venezuela in the movie, but filmed in North Africa). No sub-titles, of course, but they weren't really necessary.

Our old friends, Denis and Dominique Constancias, invited us to lunch at their house in Montfavet with Richard and Nicole Stiel, who live in Uzès near the ancient Roman aqueduct at Pont du Gard over which we've walked with hearts in our mouths on several occasions. I need not add a word about the quality of the food and wine. Dee-lish, as they used to say in the Brooklyn. That was on a Sunday, the day of the second round of the French presidential election, where they do things differently from the American way: at precisely 20:00 hours the results are announced on the TV, no prolonged blabber by "anchors" or exit polls or any of the hoopla buildup that accompanies the circus of elections here. No information about the course of the voting prior to that time. Then, of course, the talking heads comment on the results, with each political party represented by a spokesman to give the official line.

Not to be outdone, the Stiels invited us to dinner at their house along with two other couples whom we had not met previously, all semi-retired in the south and all well read, cultured people with flair and elegance in their speech and dress. A pleasure to be with them, especially since we don't travel in suit-and-tie company here in Key West, where the cultured intellectual class wears shorts and t-shirts!

At some point in one's sojourns in Provence one comes across Freddie Mistral, as inevitably as the appearance of a blister on one's toe after walking with new leather shoes. The experiences with Mistral are less painful than a toe blister and indeed can be quite pleasant, instructive, and sometimes amusing. Frédéric Mistral (1830-1914), winner of the Nobel Prize for literature in 1904,[33] this poet, ethnologist and playwright, whose physical similarities with Buffalo Bill Cody did not go unnoticed when the latter visited France with his circus, was a founding member of the Félibrige, an organization devoted to the preservation of the traditional language (Provençal) and culture of the Languedoc region. Indeed, he wrote and published his works in that language and translated some of them into French for the more commercial publishers in Paris. With his Nobel money he endowed the ethnographic museum in Arles, a repository one can still visit with profit and pleasure, although the last time we visited some years ago dust had settled over the artifacts and dioramas. I'm told they have been cleaned since then.[34]

---

[33] Mistral, whose works are still studied in French schools, inexplicably shared the prize with the Spanish playwright José Echegaray (1832-1916), a mathematician-economist who founded the Bank of Spain and served as minister of finance before going into exile where he began writing more than seventy plays, which, though popular at the time, are no longer produced or studied in schools..

[34] Not much of his work has been translated into English, but see *The Memoirs of Frédéric Mistral* (1986 edition); the standard English language biography remains Richard Aldington's *Introduction to Mistral* (1956).

Somewhere I read the following story: Mistral's father lies dying and calls his son to his bedside, his hands already icy.

-- Frédéric, quel temps fait-il? the old man whispers.

-- Il pleut, mon père ...

-- Eh bien! S'il fait beau temps pour les semailles, the old man replies softly, but firmly.

Et il rendit son âme à Dieu!

Which might be translated as, "The rain is good for the seed planting. And so saying he gave up his soul to god." Or, as Chance the Gardener might say, "I understand, Ben. It is good to plant in the spring."[35]

Finally, we did get back to Tavel to look at the old place where we spent that by now unbelievable year. The Hostillerie de Tavel no longer serves food to the public, and the Auberge de Tavel (once the proud possessor of a Michelin star but that was a long time ago) was inexplicably closed. So we bought a six pack of rosé from a smiling young woman in the vineyard store in what was formerly the butcher shop on the main drag and ate at a new tiny restaurant across the street from the only bar in town and loved it. The waitressing wife and her cooking husband, as well as the other clients, proved to be friendly and gregarious. (The wine

---

[35] Chance is also known in some Washington DC circles as Chauncey Gardner. See the film *Being There* (Herbert Ross, 1979) based on the eponymous novel by Jerzy Kosinski (1971).

was so good we had to return a couple of days later to buy another batch. How we could have consumed so much of the cheap blended waste from the cooperative during our miraculous year there is a matter only explicable by citing one's age and lack of experience with rosé wines then, as compared to now when one has become an expert! No doubt the cheapness of the cost also played a major role. We would take our eleven-liter plastic container to the cooperative on the edge of the village and the clerk would stick into it a long nozzle attached to a hose anchored in an unseen vat of the blend from several vineyards and pump the plonk until the container was full, much like the station attendant pumped gas into our dilapidated Peugeot sedan. At home we decanted the wine into bottles and corked them tightly. We had only a mini fridge so could not put the bottles there to cool, which was fine in the winter, but during the summer we had to drink the stuff fairly rapidly before it went off. Now we buy only bottles from the chateaux, much higher quality, much higher price.)

After ten sunny and productive days, we took the train to Paris where the Stiels had generously put their apartment at our disposal and where we were to meet two friends from Key West, Di Young and Luke Wright. We arrived more or less on time, but no friends awaiting us in the Place de la Sorbonne as planned. We put our baggage in the Stiels' apartment just down the street from the Place and returned to the square to drink a beer and eat a sandwich. Whilst engaged in this pleasurable pursuit, we watched the organizers of a demonstration set up tables and (alas) a loudspeaker system: Vegans on the march! Still no Di and Luke. Back at the apartment Lynn-Marie could not get through to the Paris airline office to see if their plane was delayed (a matter of consistently misdialing the number, I fear), so she called her mother in St. Paul, Minnesota, to have her call the airline and find out the scoop, so to speak. Which she of course did and called back thirty minutes later to inform us that the time of arrival we had was wrong. In the end, though, it did not matter what time we had since the plane had made an emergency stop in Raleigh, North Carolina, to disembarque a dying person, which meant that unfortunate's luggage had to be found and removed, which took a long time. Not knowing this we waited and hoped they would finally show up. At one point I looked out the window down the four floors to the street and there was Di about to yell her lungs out up to the apartment window hoping we would be there to hear her. Hurrying down the stairs, we discovered Luke sitting surrounded by their luggage in the middle of the raucous vegetarians' demonstration discussing with the waiter the possible order of a large cheeseburger, to in effect thumb his nose at the demonstrators. In the end, no cheeseburger was ordered but we did have a couple of beers before stowing their luggage in the apartment and wandering off to the Bouillon Racine for a late but filling dinner of cuisine flamande and the beginning of our week in Paris.

That week seemed to disappear in a rush of blurred images. I did, however, learn how to play hearts and cribbage. We ate lunch at the Rotonde, Di and Luke spent a night in Deauville, Lynn-Marie and I visited our artist friend from Denmark, Grethe Knudsen, in her studio, had dinner with Gregory Masurovsky and Antide Champagne de Labriolle,[36] ate marinated cold haricots verts with white wine in the Café de Flore, motored down the Seine in a bateau mouche (a sight-seeing boat), spent an hour in a rather posh flea market at the Place de la Bastille (Luke is a great fan of yard sales), went through a huge, exhausting but of necessity fascinating exhibition on Surrealism at the Centre Pompidou, strolled through the Musée d'art et d'histoire du Judaïsme where an exhibition traced the development stages in Chagall's work on the windows for the synagogue of the Hadassah Hospital in Jerusalem, and, finally, Lynn-Marie and I spent four hours at lunch in a small Moroccan restaurant (Degrés de Notre Dame) with

[36] For more about whom, see "Travels in Greece and France During Three Weeks in June and July 2003: A Letter," elsewhere in this volume.

a former colleague of hers from Cambridge (Mass.) now living in Paris just off the Quai Montebello (couscous avec saucisson et mashed pommes de terre). We left for Corfu with full bellies and whirling brains.

The wait at the new Athens airport for the flight to Corfu was of such duration that we thought we should have brought along sleeping bags and a tent. The fact that this was not the old Athens airport, but rather the new one constructed in time for the 2004 Olympic Games at minimally 50% above original cost estimates, did not mitigate the length of annoyed time we spent, but in the end the Olympic Airlines airplane did take off, late of course. So we were able to meet our responsibilities to the Durrell School of Corfu, on which board of directors and faculty I serve.[37]

The 2002 School session began with a two-day symposium introduced by Richard Pine, the School's founder and academic director, entitled "Understanding Misunderstanding," a theme generated by the increase in intensity and violence of what has come to be called "the clash of civilizations." It is unfortunate that many of those who committed to giving papers cancelled at the last moment so we ended with four of us who made presentations with the audience of twenty-

---

[37] For a history of the School and its purposes, see "The Durrell School of Corfu," below.

135

five or thirty auditors who eagerly participated in the lively discussions.[38]

The schedule for the School itself had to be somewhat modified as well because not as many students signed up for the seminars as anticipated. All the post-September 11, 2001 anxieties we subsume in the phrase "fear of flying" no doubt is the root cause of this phenomenon. Consequently, my seminar on European culture between the wars was cancelled and I joined the seminar on the art of biography led by Ian MacNiven, the authorized biographer of Lawrence Durrell, in which I played the comfortable role of number one kibitzer. This seminar took place in the large auditorium of the grand old building housing the Corfu Reading Society and its library situated at the end of Kapodistriou Street above the sea. If one could wish for an ideal research library facility, this might be at the top of the list.

Despite the defections, thirty-seven interested souls from twelve countries and continents participated in the lectures, seminars and field classes. One of the highlights of the first week (Lynn-Marie and I could not stay for the second and final week) was undoubtedly the performances of the traditional Karaghiozis shadow theater. Remotely similar to a Punch and Judy show in that

---

[38] The four were R. Pine, Elemer Hankiss of the Hungarian Academy of Sciences, John Brandon of the Asia Foundation in Washington, D.C., and your author.

puppets on sticks act out the story line in a small box-like theater set-up behind which the puppeteers stand to manipulate the characters and speak the lines. The plots of the performances vary considerably, often with political themes, but the technique is always slapstick. The most famous operator of the Karaghiozis is Eugenio Spatharis, whose father operated the performance the Durrell family attended in 1937.[39]   Mr. Spatharis, at the age of 78, gave two energetic performances of the show at the Old Fortress on the eastern promontory east of the Esplanade, one for the Durrell School and another for children of all ages from the island, funded by a grant the School obtained from the Coca-Cola Hellenic Bottling Company and supported by the Municipality of Corfu. The children roared with laughter and bent over with giggles because they, of course, could understand the language, which most from the School could not. As a result of the support provided by the Hellenic Bottling Company, the Durrell School video taped the performance and distributed copies to every school on the island.

As we have come to expect when being on Corfu, we indulged ourselves in food and wine, the

---

[39]For a graphic description of this performance, see the relevant chapter in Lawrence Durrell, *Prospero's Cell* (1945 and recent editions) and the article, "The Durrell School of Corfu," elsewhere in this volume.

consumption of which with friends and colleagues constituted one of the great pleasures of our stay. I remember particularly the breakfasts in the garden of the Bella Venezia Hotel with James Nichols and Susan and Ian MacNiven, meals that positively bubbled with energetic laughter and ideas for projects so far fetched that at the end of the day we smiled at our own audacity.

So it is understandable that we did not want to leave the island, but our time was ebbing away so we heeded the schedule and flew to Athens, the last stop on this magical trip. Several things remain clear in the mind about the two days in the Greek capital: the horrid traffic, the wonderful view of the city from the terrace of the newly renovated Benaki Museum where we had coffee in the café after admiring the artifacts on exhibition, the dinners of so many flavors at the home of our friends Aphrodite and Yannis Papastephanou, the exhibition of works from the permanent collection at the National Gallery, the huge fantastic futurist sculpture of a running man that dominates the intersection where the Hilton Hotel looms across the street from the National Gallery, and the peaceful green gardens and sprawling beige stone edifice housing the Gennadis Library (in some ways a larger version of the Corfu Reading Society building, both ideal places to conduct research or simply enjoy the small exhibitions of art and documents on the walls in cooler temperatures than outside in the streets).

All things we look back on as marvelously unprecedented must come to an end, and so it was with this trip. We flew to Paris and pleasured ourselves with a fish dinner on the sidewalk at La Méditerranée on the Place de l'Odéon in Paris where we once again stayed overnight at the Delavigne, a small hotel off the Place de l'Odéon, around the corner from the street where the bookshops of Sylvia Beach and Adrienne Monnier made literary history. The flight to Miami was uneventful, an unusual phenomenon in the age of mass tourism, and we deeply appreciated the brilliance of Lynn-Marie's decision that we stay in the Miami airport hotel after arriving at 8:45 in the evening. We timed our departure the following day to reach Snappers waterside restaurant on Key Largo at the lunch hour. Grilled fish sandwiches, pommes frites, and several Coronas later we drove on down the keys to the southernmost point in the nation and home, taking our memories with us, and anticipating next summer.

Épisode quotidien chez Mme Moure

The unnamed kitten, too small to
withstand the mistral's galvanic force
tumbles joyfully in the wind-torn yard,
head over paws, wind-blown, happy.

Then the hysterical mutt races in pursuit,
intentions unclear but threatening;
Micheline plunges into the wind
muttering dialect Italian curses
accompanied by Madame's panic cries,

"Finette! Finette! Finette!"
which the screaming dog ignores.

Stooping, Micheline gently cuddles the
      kitten,
curses soothing into a form of cooing,
and kicks at the dog leaping at her bulk.

The mistral's chilly whoomp
leaves the sun its yellow brilliance,
but blows askew the balance of
olive trees, animals and human beings.

(Tavel, 3.VIII.1983

140

The Question of Salade Niçoise: A Brief Discourse

SALADE NIÇOISE is one of those eclectic composed salads about which everyone has an opinion as to which ingredients are allowed and which are definitely not. A random sample of cookbooks on our groaning shelves provides information, often contradictory, proffered at times with an assurance of correctness bordering on the sanctimonious.

Why not start with the volume most often to be found in American kitchens in recent times: the Rombauers make two wise statements about the matter, to wit: the recipe "is often carried to the point of agreeable anarchy, when it becomes a salmagundi" and the cautionary "In compounding keep in mind the law of diminishing returns."

(Having known the word "salmagundi" all my adult life, and having from time to time read the literary magazine of that name, it came as something of a shock to learn I did not know its meaning. I had always vaguely thought of it as the name for some small lizard-like creature native to the American southwestern deserts. But what would this animal have to do with a French tuna salad? So I looked it up in Webster's 2nd edition of 1951 to find: "1. A mixed dish, as of chopped meat and pickled herring, with oil, vinegar, pepper, and onions. 2. Hence, a heterogeneous mixture: a medley; potpourri." The meat and herring reference led me first to believe the editors of this Webster edition harbor a negative attitude toward a salmagundi, and I must admit it stopped me for a moment, until I recalled how tasty a good Labskaus is!)

The Rombauers then give a minimalist version, close to Escoffier's, but without the tunny fish, which includes tomatoes, cucumber, anchovies, black olives, bibb lettuce, and romaine with a vinaigrette dressing.[40] Given the "average American" audience for this marvelous source of culinary knowledge, it is not surprising that garlic is dealt with by rubbing the salad bowl with a small piece of it.

The intrepid Elizabeth David, in her indispensable *French Provincial Cooking*, gives Escoffier's recipe as "Tunny fish in oil, the flesh of tomatoes, diced anchovy fillets. Seasoning of tarragon, chervil and chopped chives, with or without mustard." Note that although one reads time and again that small, pitted black olives are an absolute necessity for salade niçoise, Escoffier, who was born and bred in the Midi, does not

---

[40]Who among us knows that a "vinegarroon" is a whip scorpion in Mexico and the southwestern United States, "which is popularly believed to be venomous; - so called from the odor it emits when alarmed." Now we know.

142

include them. So much for the power of authority. Personally, I am distraught that he rejects garlic, without which, like wine, I can barely get through the day.

As Mrs. David notes, Heyraud's *La Cuisine à Nice* demands young artichoke hearts, black olives, raw sweet peppers, tomatoes, and anchovy fillets, with a seasoning of olive oil, vinegar, salt, pepper, mustard, and fines herbes – no tunny or garlic at all. And surely the mustard-vinegar combination tends to cancel the piquancy of the fines herbes?

It is both reasonable and practical to go about determining the ingredients, "proper" or not, based on when the salad will be served. Despite her august and well-deserved reputation as a food writer, Mrs. David is not exempt from making definitive statements that are foolish, such as the salade niçoise "is always served as an hors-d'oeuvre." She is not alone in this, to be sure. A pamphlet masquerading as a book, by Gerald Clayton, called *Looking and Cooking in Provence* (1974) tells us flatly "No cooked vegetables of any kind should appear in a salade niçoise, nor should any lettuce," and "The tomatoes should always be quartered, never sliced."[41] Ah, those eccentric English. My advice is to always be suspicious of, and never fail to maintain a certain distance from,

---

[41]One might note here that Escudier, in *La Véritable Cuisine Provençal et Niçoise*, slices his tomatoes for the salad.

any salad recipe that uses the words "never" and "always."

If the salad is to be served as a first course, it makes sense to keep it as simple as possible, but if it is to be the main course of the meal, it makes equal sense to add some substance to the plate. For example, we have not mentioned as yet additional ingredients, which are often part of the recipe: boiled (waxy) potatoes, hard-cooked eggs, green string beans (haricots vertes), and capers, although if anchovies are in the mix, what do capers contribute?

Miss Alice Toklas, who spent much time in Haute-Provence at the foot of the Alps, uses both diced potatoes and diced green beans, with the warning "Do not overcook." Very good advice, indeed. Mix with a vinaigrette of olive oil, lemon juice, salt and pepper, form into a mound and sprinkle with anchovies, black olives, capers and fresh chopped basil. Add quartered, peeled tomatoes around the edge of the plate. This is very close to our own standard version.

The redoubtable James Beard allows the salad to be served as a main course for lunch and agrees that variations are perfectly in order for variety and to take advantage of seasonal vegetables. He also includes Boston or romaine lettuce – which some people, including Lynn-Marie and me – find inappropriate, and would permit a large assortment of raw veg. He does note that many of these are optional, which we hope is another way of saying use only a few of these as they are available, not all of them at the same time. Beard adds onion to the mix, about which see below in our own recipe. Before we offer that, however, let us look at two French sources, which seems only fair when considering this eminently French dish, although some ancient Niçoise might dispute the "French" part of that description.

Florence de Andreis writes in her *La Cuisine provençale d'aujourd'hui* (1980) for the widest possible spectrum of readers, which is to be welcomed if this means a broad variety of different recipes. In this case, unfortunately, it means a recipe for salade niçoise containing thirteen ingredients. The law of diminishing returns finds its justification here.

Finally, to show that while some dishes have been around for a long time, their names may change over time's passage. Marius Morard ("Chef de Cuisine du *Rosbif*, Ancien Elève d'Henri Campé d'Avignon, Roubion et Isard et Secrétaire de la Societé Culinaire de Marseille")[42] wrote a fascinating book called *Les Secrets de la Cuisine dévoilés*, first published in 1886 and republished in photo-mechanical format on 1988 under the title *Manuel complet de la Cuisinière Provençal*. One looks in vain for a recipe entitled "salade niçoise."

---

[42] In 1886, Le Rosbif was a well-known restaurant in Marseille with a very modern kitchen for its time.

But if one turns to the page describing "salade provençal" one discovers a recipe with some familiar ingredients, and some not usually related to the salad, combined to create what we can reasonably recognize as salade niçoise, should we wish: potatoes diced or in strips, pieces of artichoke hearts, small green beans, tarragon, green olives stuffed with anchovy, quartered hard-cooked eggs, strips of crawfish (langoustes), and a mustard vinaigrette. The substitutions for black olives and tunny fish is mildly surprising, but remains within the general paradigm. What shocks is the optional replacement of the crawfish with red beets! Morard does warn his readers to place the beets around the periphery of the other ingredients to avoid the entire salad taking on the beets' distinctive red coloring. At this point the integument has been burst asunder and we have entered into the stratosphere of (premature) nouvelle cuisine at one of its extremes.

While we, Lynn-Marie and I, do not consider ourselves to be purists or minimalists, there is a certain point beyond which we believe it is impossible to go without so corrupting the dish that it no longer can be accurately described as salade niçoise, which of course Morard did not do. In this case, however, simplicity should be the guide.

Ergo, here are the ingredients we have found to work best and how we organize them. The amounts vary with individual taste and availability.

- Cold quartered small wax potatoes cooked al dente.
- Cold green (string) beans cooked al dente.
- Flaked tuna fish (canned in oil or water depending upon the state of one's health and diet).
- Finely chopped garlic.
- Finely chopped sweet onion (spring onions, especially the green parts, are too bitter).
- Pitted black olives (always avoid the canned variety and buy fresh in available, or use Kalamatas marinating in oil)
- Chopped anchovy (this can be picked out by guests who find the taste too severe); or a tablespoon of capers.
- Scant handful of herbes de provence.
- Vinaigrette with or without mustard (use the best olive oil and red wine vinegar available; eschew such trendy stuff as balsamic vinegar; or substitute lemon/lime juice for the vinegar).

Toss these ingredients gently but thoroughly, place covered in the refrigerator for about an hour, tossing again from time to time. Before serving, add but do not toss:

- Quartered fresh tomatoes (if summer tomatoes are not available, do not use the tasteless varieties available most of the year), and
- Quartered hard-cooked eggs,
then drizzle the vinaigrette over the salad.

A true baguette, though hard to find in many places (if you are in southern Florida or its Keys, use fresh Cuban bread), and a Preston Vineyard Vin Gris (formerly "Petit Faux") rosé make this an unbeatable summer midday or evening meal, although we've been known to make the salad in the winter when the mood comes over us.

Now, about the correct ingredients for a true bouillabaisse ... Ouf!

(Washington DC, 1999)

Travels in Greece and France During Three Weeks in June and July 2003: A Letter

Cher frère Dean,

We blew the budget before we even left the country. After driving the rental car up to the Fairfield Inn at the Miami airport we decided to have dinner at a favorite restaurant in Coral Gables: Le Provençal on the Miracle Mile. Despite the annoyance of a couple of smokers[43] and a loud table of lawyers, we enjoyably consumed a pastis with a small plate of marinated green and black olives, a bottle of Tavel rosé, veal kidneys (me) and grilled fish (Lynn-Marie), decaffeinated espresso, and paid $120, by far the most expensive meal of the entire trip. Worth every penny of it, of course, but still ...

After a typical motel breakfast (exceptionally, the coffee is quite good) accompanied by loud Miami-Cuban pop music at poolside, we drove to the Bass Museum in Miami Beach to see the Hannelore Bacon collages exhibit. She made many interesting pieces, rather under the influence of Kurt Schwitters, but more than a dozen or so of them were too much and indicated the limits of the

---

[43] Shortly thereafter the Florida state legislature passed a law banning smoking inside restaurants, for which passage we are all grateful.

genre: they all blended into a single piece that, in the end, brought on boredom. We discovered to our surprise that the museum's permanent collection holds a Rubens and a Botticelli, though why should we be surprised to find such things in Miami Beach when a private collection in Krakow holds a beautiful Leonardo painting called "Lady with Ermine"? An attempt to visit the Wolfsonian Museum in South Miami Beach failed: it closes on Wednesdays, of course, just the day we were there.

Eventually we made our way to the airport and plowed through the chaos at the Lufthansa counter; not as chaotic and impenetrable as Luxor airport in Egypt, but sufficiently disorganized to make one wonder about the vaunted German discipline and efficiency. To compensate for that stress, we ate lunch at a window seat in the airy and friendly airport restaurant and listened to the mélange of Haitian Creole, French, Spanish and occasional English phrases punctuated with bursts of dark laughter coming from the kitchen and waiters' stand nearby.

The flight from Miami to Frankfurt seemed endless, a nightmare of cramped claustrophobia, exhaustion without the ability to sleep, dinner served much too early (barely eatable, helped by the wine, which the airlines in economy no longer dispense with such liberality as in the past: soon they'll begin charging for it). I sat in the middle for much of the trip, next to a very nervous, tobacco-deprived young Lithuanian (or Russian), a nice enough fellow but consumed by spasms of nervous ticks: as soon as we got off the plane at Frankfurt he headed for a smoking area (not enclosed but located throughout the airport). Greek chaos reigned at the boarding gate, but the flight to Athens passed without any untoward event and the good lunch with red wine was served at 10:30 am, not a moment too soon, justifying our decision not to eat breakfast on the trans-Atlantic flight.

The patina of newness has not yet been worn away from the Athens airport, far outside the city, a long and expensive taxi ride away. Next time we will take the bus and subway, the latter of which is promised to be completed by the time of the summer Olympics next year. There are many in Greece who smile knowingly at the idea.[44]

The Hotel Plaka is appropriately enough smack in the middle of the Plaka, the oldest part of the city situated beneath the Acropolis and the Parthenon, and our room offered a magnificent view of both in the evening light filtered through the light miasma of automobile exhaust pollution. We were reminded of another visit to Athens some twenty years ago, when we stayed at a cheap hotel in the Plaka where we went to dinner with our

---

[44] With typical Mediterranean inventiveness the subway did finally run from the airport to downtown Athens by mid-summer 2004, but only by leaving several stations on the line unfinished.

German friend, Heiner Adamsen and his sail boat crew, an evening that ended in the minuscule bar at our hotel. As tiny as it was, a plentiful supply of that highly dangerous Greek brandy, Metaxas, fueled conversation far later than was prudent. As a consequence, the following morning when picking up the rental car I immediately ran into a truck just in front of us in the parking lot, mistaking drive for reverse. Fortunately, we'd just gotten the relevant insurance and the left headlight was swiftly replaced. Unfortunately, the sea we crossed on the ferry to Evia was quite choppy that morning.

The Hotel Plaka is but a short walk from Syntagma Square and the venerable, now renovated, Grande Bretagne Hotel (known to us cognoscenti simply as the GB) in whose dark wood, richly appointed bar we have spent many a pleasant, cool hour over the years. The bar, too, has been renovated and expanded, but retains its coziness, disturbed only by the ubiquitous cell phones without which so many people cannot seem to live fully satisfactory lives. Ouzo and salted nuts are so refreshing in all that elegance, where it is assumed that all the staff speaks fluent English, and so they do. Later, after stumbling around the narrow Plaka streets looking for the English-language bookshop on Nikis Street (closed of course), we sat at a table on the sidewalk in a small restaurant whose name and exact location I wish I could remember: lamb with fennel and a thin pungent sauce, fried potatoes and a tasty red plonk with a Greek salad eaten slowly, with cherubic smiles on our tired faces, meant that we would sleep well with the window open. And so it was.

Early the following morning I finished reading the poet James Merrill's *The Diblos Notebook*, his obscurantist attempt at experimental fictional prose. Fortunately it is less than 200 pages in length and now resides in the Durrell School of Corfu library; perhaps someone will read it sometime. The next day we discovered a museum we had not previously known, the Frissiras Museum of Contemporary European Art (whose title doesn't preclude the presence of a couple of American and Australian artists), in two finely renovated buildings in the Plaka. The collection contains some interesting canvases and drawings with emphasis on the representational rather than the abstract, mainly younger living artists unknown to me, including an exceptionally fine draughtsman and painter named Martinelli. I thought this museum would be a fine repository for some of our friend Gregory Masurovsky's work; so when we returned to Key West I sent Mr. Frissiras a letter with a copy of my book *A Piece of Paris*, for which Gregory provided the drawings, and some other samples of his work. We'll see what happens, if anything.[45]

One of the more fabulous art centers in Athens, the Benaki Museum, is housed in the old Benaki family residence on one of the city's main boulevards (along with various embassies, banks and the Greek Ministry of Foreign Affairs) a few blocks from Syntagma Square. It is full of a widely eclectic collection gathered by the family over the years, but more importantly for us at lunch time it has a small restaurant on a 5th floor terrace overlooking the National Gardens. A breeze is almost always blowing under the canopy, making it pleasant to sit there even on the hottest day, and summer days in Athens can be excruciatingly hot. The savage growling of the Athenian traffic is muted and the pigeons cavort in the air in front of the terrace. (When the Athens city council passed a law intended to stagger and reduce the number of cars in the city by allowing those whose license plates ended in an odd number to be in the city only every other day, those who could afford it, and there were apparently many, purchased a second car and ensured that the plate

---

[45] Gregory Masurovsky is an American artist who has lived in Paris since the mid-1950s and who illustrated my book, *A Piece of Paris. The Grand XIVth* (1996). His work with the writer Michel Butor was the subject of a major retrospective at the Pontoise Museum outside Paris in the autumn of 2004 covering the thirty years of their collaboration. More about Gregory can be found further on in this letter. Neither Mr. Frissiras nor his staff ever responded to my letter and gift.

ended in an odd number, thus defeating the purpose of the law. Once again creative action inspired by egotistical indifference foils an attempt to clear the air.)

There is nothing quite so *satisfying* as a flavorful but light meal at midday when one has tired of walking through hot streets and cool museums: the waiter brings a basket of warm bread and a small jar of herbed butter and thoughtfully accepts your order of mineral water, a Greek salad, a chicken salad sandwich and a carafe of cool white wine of unknown but honest vintage. Indeed, he seems to actually *approve* of the order, and hastens off to fulfill it.

That afternoon we spent a long time in the Cyclades Museum admiring the work of those artists 3000 years ago. Later, we had a drink at our friend Aphrodite's apartment before descending the neighborhood steps (much like those in Montmartre) to a local restaurant she has patronized for twenty-five years. Sitting outside, practically on the steps, I ate the best grilled meat in years – no fish in this eatery – along with zucchini in lemon and oil, spinach or dandelion stalks in lemon and oil, deep fried eggplant (actually quite light and tasty), the ubiquitous Greek salad and the owner's own red wine. Bouf!

The following day we drove with Aphrodite out to her summer apartment on the long curving island of Evia, about two and a half hours from

Athens, sometimes crawling through tiny villages where you wouldn't think two cars going in opposite directions could actually pass each other. Hair-raising is the appropriate description. Aphrodite's friend, Maria, came with us for the day; turns out she has a design firm that did the uniforms and dresses for the GB staff, an accomplishment for which she is justifiably proud. We swam in water calmer but colder than our own Key West beach at Fort Zachary Taylor, known affectionately by locals as Fort Zack. Aphrodite ordered grilled fish take out for lunch, which we consumed with gusto and local white wine to the sounds of the Emperor Concerto, allegro molto. That evening Maria took a taxi back to Athens (not cheap at about $65) and at ten o'clock we wandered across the lane to Stephanos and Katy's place for dinner, which actually didn't get served until close midnight. Everyone speaks English to some extent and their children all seem to have studied in England or the USA. Much of the meal I theoretically should not have eaten (especially the gorgeous grilled sausages), but I did and too much of it. The wine flowed, of course. We left an hour after midnight, but some of the women stayed up playing cards until 3:00 in the morning. No one seems to read at the summer place, though I talked to Stephanos, a retired chemist in the tanning industry, about Orlando Figes' books on the culture of Russia and the Soviet Union that he's read in English. Perhaps they only read when in Athens during the winter.

Ninety-seven degrees in Athens, but on Evia in the village of Vathia a breeze flows through the house by the water that makes the heat bearable. Nonetheless, I slept poorly, but was able to write some notes for the second volume of the Berlin novel I seem to have been writing for ten years now. The lack of exercise, the volume of food, the temperature and what some would consider too much wine filled my brain with wool and rendered me physically lethargic. The hour or two long late afternoon naps are supposed to compensate for this, but in my case they make matters worse. Tant pis pour moi. We drove back to Athens arriving about 10:00 in the evening and after Aphrodite dropped us off in the Plaka we found an outdoor restaurant for a small supper with a drinkable white wine; we became quite fond of tzazikis, and ate it at every opportunity, making it as ubiquitous as the Greek salad.

Monday we walked halfway across the city to check on the National Art Museum: closed for Pentecost, as were all the other museums and some of the restaurants (including the Benaki where we'd planned to eat lunch), so we trudged back to the Plaka and found a cool garden restaurant called the Kalisto where we had a pleasant, shady, well-watered late lunch. Several tables away a mixed race couple sat down for a bottle of wine and something to eat. My notebook has the following entry about them: "Durrell character (bestimmt French) w black woman. Does he look like one of the brothers or like a character in one of their books? Je ne sais pas."[46]

Then it was time to head for the airport in a taxi, where, knowing we would arrive on Corfu too late and tired to eat dinner, we sat in the newly opened restaurant to nibble some bread and tzazikis and sip white wine while we laughed at the foibles of French tourists thinking everyone in Europe should speak French, or in an extreme case English. On the island two kilometers from the coast of Albania the Durrell School of Corfu, on whose board of directors and faculty I serve, awaited us.[47]

We landed that night at 10:30 and checked in to a small corner room at the Konstantinopoulis Hotel on the old harbor. One fascinating characteristic of this pleasant hostelry is the inescapable presence of birds. The darting swifts dominate the sky around the hotel and above the harbor,

---

[46] One does like to parade one's knowledge of other languages from time to time, it is true. Nonetheless, it is also true that at certain moments in the course of jotting down a passing thought or event words in various languages come to mind as perfect expressions of one's thoughts. Generations ago, in the age of true education of the deserving elite, these thoughts would be expressed in Latin or Greek phrases. Today we who are, alas, ignorant of the classics, make do with those languages currently in use.

[47] See "The Durrell School of Corfu," elsewhere in this volume for a fuller account of the School and its history.

ceaselessly wheeling and swooping in short arcs and long, their cries piercing the air (we assume the sounds are joyful), their wings pedaling faster than the eye can blink.

We quickly unpacked and a few minutes later we walked to the Liston (the esplanade side of the French-built long buildings with arcades mirroring those along the rue de Rivoli in Paris) to sit under the trees in our favorite café, the Olympia, with a glass of wine to watch the locals promenading with their small children scurrying about at the top of their lungs at midnight. We slept well despite the noise from the street in front of the hotel. The primitive air conditioner worked fine and not too loudly so we used it and closed the windows to keep out the noise when it became a hindrance to sleep. The ability to sleep soundly is important when one's days are filled with various kinds of physical and mental activities requiring large amounts of energy. This truism becomes all the more true as one ages.

We stayed on Corfu for eight warm, sunny days filled with the intellectual stimulation of the daily seminars and field classes at the School and the physical satisfactions of food and wine (and a lot of water every day to make up for the dehydration caused by the climate) and constant walking.

At 7:00 or 7:30 each evening we walked to the Olympia for a glass of wine and viewing the people before dinner, which we did not get to until

9:30 or so. Often one or another colleague from the School would come by and join us. Because we ate all meals in restaurants we tried to go to a different one each time, although we did have a couple of favorites, especially one near the old harbor called Moraghia, which means "sea walls" in Greek, where the grilled lemon chicken with saffron rice lifted the act of dining to transcendental heights of gustatory delight. The carafes of local plonk, whether red or white, are also very drinkable.

One night we made the mistake of eating in a restaurant where one goes into the kitchen to choose the fish which one wishes to eat. All very well and good, and very finely done, but we had momentarily forgotten that fresh fish on Corfu is a rare delicacy, the price of which reflects the rarity of the item in question. Since the waters in the Ionian Sea are largely fished out, fresh fish is imported at great cost, which of course is passed on to the consumer. The cost of the meal was a surprising 70 Euros. That was the first and last time such a thing happened on this trip. And a year later, the Ashcrofts and Richard Pine introduced us to two funky tavernas, one north, the other south of Corfu Town, which served fresh fish, grilled to perfection, at more than reasonable prices. So it can be done, but not likely in the center of the city.

Corfu Town is much like Key West without the large gay population or the affronts along the lower end of Duval Street filled with great gobs of tourists and vulgar t-shirt shops.[48] The cruise ships are not as gargantuan as those that infest the waters of the Caribbean and the piers at Key West, but there are more of them plying their offensive trade through the channel separating the island from the Albanian mainland. To escape this horror, one could live in a village elsewhere on the island and come into town whenever necessary by bus or car, but this would be to give in to a hideous result of modern technological "progress."

The Durrell School of Corfu rents a large five-room apartment as an office-library-study center on the (European) first floor of a building of fairly ancient vintage in the middle of the bustling bazaar section of Corfu Town. The rooms are spacious and airy and the library includes three editions of the Encyclopaedia Britannica, all of the Durrells' works, books by the School's faculty on a wide range of subjects, volumes on the Ionian Islands, modern literature in English, and Hellenic civilization and culture in addition to a collection of some of Lawrence Durrell's manuscripts and other documents in photocopy that Richard Pine, the School's founder and academic director, and

---

[48] Sad to say in 2004 we spotted one of these egregious insults to the civilized mind and eye on a Corfu Town street populated by tourist stores. Globalization has a lot to answer for.

161

others have collected as they researched various aspects of Durrell's life and work. We spent a pleasant afternoon there with the group (the participants at this year's reduced session numbered fourteen, the right size for a largish seminar)[49] talking about everything including Michelangelo, sipping wine and munching on the lavish layout of snacks lying invitingly on several tables and windowsills throughout the rooms.

Lynn-Marie and I refrained from munching because we had eaten a fair-sized lunch in the mountains at the northern end of the island where we traveled in a rental car to see the coastline. Discovering that the villages along the coast all had been (over)developed into little mass tourism meccas (Mister Kurtz's horror statement well fits the situation), we left the shoreline and drove inland around a seemingly unending series of hairpin curves, a task which challenges dexterity and the tendency to vertigo, until at the crux of one of them there stood the Paradise restaurant with a magnificent view of the green valley plain below in the shadow of the mountain called Pantokrator. The food was mediocre (the large chunks of feta tasted the blandest and the wine was the worst sour liquid we had during the Corfu sojourn, bordering

---

[49] Due to the continuing residual effects of the terrorist attacks on New York City and the Pentagon in September 2001, the School deferred its full 2003 program until the following year, but offered a five-day session of seminars and field classes.

on the undrinkable; we left half of it in the carafe). The view made up for the so-so food, but nothing could make up for the bad wine. An elderly German couple with their 40ish daughter arrived and walked stolidly to a table near us. That is, the parents walked in such a manner, the daughter still dressed in her nightclub clothes (dress fairly falling off the upper part of her body and highly heeled sandals) staggered somewhat, but made it to the table, where they talked banalities about missed flights and the incomprehensible strangeness of Greek food. The smell of herbs and dry heat rolled gently in waves up from the valley.

A second reason we ignored the delectable-looking hors d'oeuvres at the School's library was the fact that later that evening we planned to eat the best "roast lamp" on the island with stuffed green peppers and a good wine sitting at tables in the street at the Chrysomalis restaurant near the Liston where we've eaten over the years without ever suffering less than well-cooked, fine-tasting meal. (The night before we had eaten what pretended to be grilled "lamp chops" at another restaurant, but were mainly grizzle and fat, during which a piece of my permanent bridgework broke off, a sure sign indicating one ought not to return to that particular eatery.) The spelling of the meat is an accurate transcription of the way it is spelled on most Corfiot menus.

The School's academic sessions were held in the Art Café garden overlooking the bay that separates Corfu from the Albanian coast and the island of Vidos. It is a most pleasant setting and we moved the tables from time to time to stay in the shade as the sun followed its arching path across the bright blue sky. Each day we tackled different themes, which included globalization and nationalism (using Durrell's *Revolt of Aphrodite* [*Tunc* and *Nunquam*] and Iain Banks' *The Business* as spring boards), translation – not just from one language to another but the whole spectrum of cultural and political mores, following a definition of the word that reaches beyond the usual mundane one to include the matter of how one translates one culture into another, but does not slight the debate over how one best translates prose, and more particularly poetry (which many poets and scholars have said cannot be done at all) – post-colonialism, and reading cultural landscapes. Under the rubric "Reading Cultural Landscapes in North-Eastern Corfu" the group departed by bus in the morning for the small village of Episkepsi, which contains remnants of 400-year-old architecture styles embedded in more modern renovations. David Ashcroft, who with his wife Alexina, the School's administrative director, has lived in a small village in the area for years, guided the participants through the village and talked about the changes brought about in the villagers' way of life as well as the manner in which they constructed their houses. The bus then moved the group further inland to the almost deserted village of Old Perithia, now the home of a few shepherds and, on weekends, of several wealthy people who are restoring some of the old stone buildings. After a fine lunch of local food and drink at one of the two small restaurants on the edge of the village, Mr. Ashcroft told the group about the history of the village dating back to the time of the barbarian pirates and the reasons for its desertion by the inhabitants approximately 25 years ago.

My contribution to the curriculum was a morning seminar on the subject of the writer in exile, emphasizing the difference between exile (involuntary departure under duress when faced with prison or death) and emigration (voluntary departure due to dislike of a regime's ideology and practice). The problems of writers suddenly at large in a new and previously unknown culture, and, most importantly, a new language and audience, formed the substance of the discussion.

The group used one of the mornings at the Art Café garden to engage in a wide-ranging discussion of the general phenomenon of post-colonialism and its multitude of meanings, swerving from the absurdly incomprehensible to the acutely relevant. Since this was Monday, though the garden remained open to the public the café was closed: it is owned and operated by the city and Monday is "strike" day for some city employees, so the staff did not show up for work. We brought our own water and did not suffer thereby, though some of us missed the delicious coffee frappés normally served by the staff.

The afternoon seminar was devoted to a discussion led by James Gifford of Lawrence Durrell's essay "Oil for the Saint: A Return to Corfu" and the various ways this "recorso" can be interpreted in the light of post-colonial and other theories.

On the School's final evening, Mrs. Sylvia Dimitriadis Steen, owner of the Silva Estate where she is breeding the endangered miniature Skyros ponies, generously provided supper for the participants and a grand time was had by all, even those who had flights out early the next morning. This was a rare opportunity to enjoy dinner in "Durrellian" surroundings and stroll through the well-kept gardens to be astounded by the spectacular views over Kanoni and the south of the island. Mrs. Steen is a great animal lover and when she greeted us at the beginning of the evening two dogs and a sheep accompanied her. The sheep followed her everywhere, in the house, around the gardens, on the terrace where we ate. Sylvia said that because she had gotten the sheep when it was a week or so old it thought she was its mother and rarely left her side. Sylvia ruefully murmured that she would, of course, have to wean the beast away from this curiously un-animal behavior pattern.

The lengthy and exquisitely prepared dinner consisted of a dozen different dishes, including a fresh red snapper grilled by Dave Ashcroft especially for me and Emilie Pine, PhD student at Trinity College Dublin and daughter of Richard, formerly an assistant bartender with Susan MacNiven and me at the 1992 Avignon Durrell conference in the Palais des Papes, when she was all of fourteen years of age.[50] Dave remembered that I prefer fish to redmeat and that Emilie is a vegetarian. Marvelous. Somehow great jugs of red and white wine kept appearing throughout the dinner, and Mrs. Steen most generously drove those of us staying at the Konstantinopoulis down to the harbor, none quite sober, except her magnanimous self.

The next day, a massive hangover accompanying me like a beaten dog, we flew to Frankfurt where we had a four-hour wait for the plane to Paris, but having had a fine airline meal

---

[50] Needless to say we allowed her only an occasional sip of the product we dispensed with such élan and laughter. In October 2004, Miss Pine brilliantly defended her dissertation before her doctoral committee at Trinity College Dublin before she flew to Java to study the dance for several months.

with red wine for lunch on the way from Athens, we weathered the time fairly well. We could have gotten to Paris on an earlier flight but the Lufthansa gate personnel refused to be bothered with the paperwork. So by the time we got to the apartment on the rue Cardinal Lemoine, the clock had struck midnight; happy to be in the city, we collapsed and slept soundly until mid-morning. On the way to a late breakfast at a café on the Place Contrescarpe we passed the building containing Ernest and Hadley Hemingway's first Paris apartment, upon the wall of which is attached a plaque noting the fact with citations from the mendacities in *A Moveable Feast* (in French of course). The clothing shop on the ground floor is called "Paris est une fête" (the French title of that book), and the travel agency on the first floor boasts a sign reading "Agences des Voyages 'Under Hemingway'" – this is no joke (but of course it *is*!). The café crème and tartine au beurre tasted extremely Parisian and we slipped into our accustomed state of transcendent consciousness, grinning with satisfaction.

The window at the turn of the staircase between the first and ground floor of the apartment building opens onto a narrow tin roof protecting the door to the garden containing the garbage cans. That first day a small female doll with unkempt blonde hair and bent legs lay face down on a dishcloth atop the roof. A suicided doll? A symbol? An indication of a depressed or enraged child? The next day the doll disappeared, but the dishcloth remained as long as we occupied the apartment.

Can one ever have too much of Paris? I think a point is reached when the strong desire to return to the city diminishes; it has with me. I am not sure why, perhaps because I have an aversion these days to large urban centers, much preferring small villages for the quiet and slower pace of life. Nonetheless, after the tremendous heat of the first day (the previous three weeks had been brutal), the weather cooled off and we carried on meeting our appointments and walking all over the place. Eventually I decided my brief aversion to the city was but a moment of insanity from which I quickly recovered.

The grocery store we patronized sold Tavel rosé, which is *why* we patronized it, at somewhat reasonable prices so our first lunch in the apartment consisted of Badoit mineral water, rosé, baguette, lentil salad and roast chicken. The joy and rejoicing at the table overflowed reasonable bounds: the meal was one of those transcendental culinary events one does not soon forget. Of course we had to have a nap afterward. Thereafter we walked in the Luxembourg Garden and had a glass of wine at the Café Rostand on the Place Rostand. We won't do it again, however, since now a small glass of wine, costing elsewhere two or three Euros, cost 6.80! Bah. We ate that first night after Corfu in a Greek restaurant not far from the apartment in order not to lose the Mediterranean atmosphere we have come to feel quite at home in.

Museums in Paris in the summer are over-crowded, as everyone knows, so we passed on the Musée d'Orsay with its block-long lines, but we did revisit the Zadkine Museum, another haven of peace and quiet near the Luxembourg, descended into the Louvre to see a major retrospective of Leonardo drawings (much too crowded and a half hour wait in line to get in), as well as a small but acute exhibition of Max Ernst paintings and small sculptures at a gallery on the Avenue Matignon near the Grand Palais. The museum highlight of the visit was the fantastic Nicholas de Staël retrospective at the Centre Pompidou. The great, unfinished canvas, "Le concert," a copy of which hangs over Lynn-Marie's desk here in Key West, was the last piece in the show. When we rounded the corner and saw it, a lump of nostalgia formed in my throat and tears welled up in my eyes. We are so accustomed to seeing the huge piece in the great hall of the Château Grimaldi in Antibes that it seemed even larger and more imposing in the smaller Pompidou venue.

A number of our friends in Paris and elsewhere in France are not doing well with their health and it is unlikely we will see them again so it was good we could visit, however briefly, some of them during our week in the city.

On a happier note, we had dinner with my former Holocaust Museum colleague, Peggy Frankston, and her friend Claude Hampel, the editor of a Yiddish magazine and newsletter, in a restaurant new to us in the rue Boulard called A Mi Chemin, a small, compact, friendly place that serves superb meals at reasonable prices. The waiter will take your photograph without a hint of a condescending smirk. Monique Lebreton-Savigny, Lynn-Marie's former French teacher in Washington, now living in Nice when she's not off to China, Peru, Vietnam, Egypt, and other points on the globe, came for lunch and spent three hours telling us about her travels and showing photographs. And of course what would a visit to Paris be without an evening with Gregory Masurovsky and Antide Champagne de Labriolle. We spent an hour at his new ground floor atelier/studio apartment in Montparnasse, having a bottle of rosé and salted nuts and chatting about his recent exhibitions and their trip to Madrid for the Black Mountain College exhibit at the Reine Sophia Museum in which he has a large drawing. The exhibit catalog is massive, as they are these days; Gregory had a Spanish language edition that he generously gave to us. Very well documented and profusely illustrated, but I can say nothing about the texts.

Two days later they came to dinner at the apartment; after they left we watched a Claude Brasseur/Claude Rich Krimi (policier) on the telly but fell asleep in the middle. We did remain awake to watch a complete Maigret episode with Bruno Cramer, the current Chief Inspector on the TV series, and almost all of a 1976 Jean-Paul Belmondo adventure, *Le corps de mon ennemi*, which could be edited down by at least 30 minutes and still be rather too long; and late one night we saw part of an incredibly lengthy interview in English with the aging Woody Allen, illustrated with clips from his films. We could not stay up until the end.

For the rest, we walked a great deal, usually eating lunch out and dinner in the apartment. This is cheaper, theoretically, but when one eats lunch at the Café de Flore with a bottle of Cuvée du Ricombre – Lussac Saint Emilion (2000) accompanying a large plate of haricots verts and a Salade de Flore, well this isn't exactly fast food price levels. The Flore represented one of the finer lunches in life; it is so pleasant to sit under the eaves on the terrace to watch the tourists wander by with stunned eyes and the Parisiennes run from the rain that lightly fell sporadically throughout the afternoon. The Flore remains a place where magical things happen: the night Gerald Durrell and "a famous Egyptian novelist" (according to a waiter, which if true was almost certainly Naguib

Mahfouz) sat next to us and I did not have the social courage to lean over to tell him how much we enjoyed his books; the hilarious full lunch upstairs with my museum colleague Radu Ioanid on a dark winter day when we sat at what we decided was the usual table at which Simone de Bouvoir wrote her daily quota of words in the 1940s; the sight of our friend Abigail Sullivan's fifteen year-old Doppelgänger sitting a couple of meters away while I distractedly ate a late breakfast; and the general history of the place, as inaccurate as it may be presented in various guidebooks ("Albert Camus regularly drank absinthe with Ernest Hemingway and Richard Wright on the terrace," and the like).

There are those occasions when one wishes for nothing more elaborate than a simple omelet with pommes frites to eat in the shade in a small, unpretentious bistro out of the direct summer sun. The chances are that the search for this place will be frustrated and this was no exception. For some unknown reason(s) we just could not find what we wanted – the eateries we looked at were either too grandiose or had no unoccupied tables out of the sun. Before terminal crankiness overcame me, we settled on Le Select, not far from Gregory's atelier, and the sauvignon blanc was fine and the lunch was tasty and there were no loud-mouthed Americans near us. Sometimes the old standbys are the best.

And we discovered that there is a square in the XVIIth arrondissement at the Porte de Champerret metro station named after the American Symbolist poet Stuart Merrill (1863-1915) who lived most of his adult life in France and wrote all his work in French. As far as I know his poems have never been translated into English. He appears as Hubert in André Gide's *Paludes*.

We left the apartment at five o'clock in the morning to catch the flight to Miami, from which point we drove south toward the southernmost point in the USA, glad to be home but sad to have left places we have come to love. I will close with an anecdote about the Catholic conservative playwright, Paul Claudel, that did not make it into either of my Paris books: Claudel, is sitting in a restaurant with friends; suddenly he holds up a flaming crêpe on the end of his fork and blurts out, "And that's how Gide will burn in hell!"

(Key West, July 14, 2003)

Tavel Morning

Baking bread smells friendly
When the heat cracks walnuts softly
Muted by the iron oven door.
Café-au-lait snuggles strong and hearty
In wide-mouthed breakfast bowls
Steaming in the rain-washed air.
We smile silently without knowing why.
Summer's hinges begin to creak
As autumn pushes against the season's door.

(24.8.1983)

The Durrell School of Corfu

(For Richard Pine)

THE GREEK ISLAND OF CORFU lies some two kilometers off the Albanian coast in the blue Ionian Sea and possesses a long checkered history. Not so long but certainly checkered is the Durrell family's life during the period 1935 to 1939 when they lived in various houses there. One might with some justification say that the family's sojourn is partly responsible for the mass tourism that infests the island each summer. Two of the Durrell brothers, Lawrence and Gerald, wrote books about the place, *Prospero's Cell* (1945) and the best selling *My Family and Other Animals* (1956), respectively, both of which contain fictional elements that subtract nothing from their verisimilitude. Nor does the odd fact that Lawrence does not mention his family except for brief obscure references to his brother Leslie, and Gerald writes as if Lawrence lived with the family, leaving his wife Nancy completely out of the story, a situation no one seems to have enquired into. Indeed, Gerald continued to tell stories about Corfu in *Birds, Beasts and Relatives* (1969), *Fillets of Plaice* (1971), *Garden of the Gods* (1978), *The Picnic and Suchlike Pandemonium* (1981) and

Marrying off Mother and Other Stories (1992), all
of which are very amusing if not entirely factually
accurate historically, so to speak.[51] Lawrence also
wrote a section about Corfu in his *The Greek
Islands* (1978) and an article, "Oil for the Saint;
Return to Corfu," published in *Holiday* (October
1966).[52] They both lived to regret their
contributions to the island's desecration by the
tourist industry.[53]

In brief, the young Larry[54] convinced his wife
Nancy and his mother Louise that life on the

---

[51] For more accurate portrayals of the Durrells' lives on Corfu, see Ian
MacNiven's authorized, *Lawrence Durrell: A Biography* (1998),
Gordon Bowker, *Through the Dark Labyrinth: A Biography of
Lawrence Durrell* (rev. ed. 1998), and Douglas Botting, *Gerald
Durrell: The Authorized Biography* (1999). See also, Richard Pine,
"Nostos: The Durrells and Corfu" in *The Anglo-Hellenic Review*, No.
26 (Autumn 2002) for a brief consideration of the subject.

[52] Reprinted in Lawrence Durrell, *Spirit of Place: Letters and Essays
on Travel*, ed. Alan Thomas (1969).

[53] In 1987 the BBC filmed *My Family and Other Animals* as a series,
which fictionalized the stories even further and made the island
attractive to the millions that viewed the programs. Gerald Durrell and
his Corfu mentor, Theodore Stephanides, made a mediocre film of
Garden of the Gods in 1967. In 1975, Peter Adams for the BBC made
a documentary film, *Spirit of Place: Lawrence Durrell's Greece*, which
contains a long section with the author returning to Corfu. Since then,
Emma Tennant has published a memoir, *A House in Corfu* (2001) and
Robert Dessaix a novel intriguingly titled *Corfu: A Novel* (2001), with
the Australian theater personality Kester Berwick as an unseen but
powerful presence. All of this kind of thing adds to the attraction of the
place and brings even more tourists. For an off-the-wall appreciation
of the island resulting from a visit there in 1920 by the poet H. D., see
the appropriate sections of her book *Tribute to Freud* (1956).

[54] Following Ian MacNiven's usage of the familiar "Larry" instead of
the more formal and distancing "Durrell" in his biography of the writer,
many Durrellians also refer to him as Larry when gathered amongst

---

sunny, warm Greek island would be so much cheaper than in gray, rainy, cold Bournemouth on the English Channel. The financial aspect of the consideration was important because the income derived from the family's investments had shrunk due to careless investing by Mrs. Durrell. And so the family took the plunge and made the move. They arrived on the overnight ferry from Brindisi, the Italian port, a civilized method of transport now rarely used by tourists and travelers alike who seem to lack the time for such amenities and so seat themselves in the cramped tube of an airplane, a transportation as ubiquitous as it is uncomfortable – unless one flies first class, of course.

Larry and Nancy traveled a couple of weeks before the rest of the family and lived in several places on the island, but for the longest period in the small bay that clasps the village of Kalami in its sometimes fierce, sometimes gentle grasp, in a house now known as The White House, directly at the water's edge. Here the ambitious writer created poems, shorter prose pieces and the now famous *The Black Book*, so explosively obscene in 1938 that it had to be published in Paris by Henry Miller's publisher, Jack Kahane's Obelisk Press. The rest of the family, mother Louise, brothers

themselves in less than solemn enclave. Gerald Durrell's widow Lee Durrell refers to him in public and private as Gerry, and we will follow her example.

Leslie and Gerry and sister Margo, lived in a succession of houses Gerry dubbed The Strawberry Pink Villa, the Daffodil-Yellow Villa, and the Snow-White Villa.[55] The entire crew left Corfu as war threatened to spread its ugly tentacles into Greece in 1939, Nancy and Lawrence to Athens, where their daughter Penelope was born, and Kalamata in the southern Peloponnesus where they precariously remained until April 1941 when the German military advance forced them to flee to Egypt by way of Crete. The rest of the family except Margo, who remained for months on Corfu, traveled in June 1939 to the relative safety of England. Larry and Gerry and their wives returned to the island separately and together on several occasions after the war.

With regard to the island itself, a list of the countries and empires that occupied Corfu at various times offers a foretaste of the characteristics that make the place unique among Greek islands, despite the incursions of the current wave of homogenizing "globalization": the Greeks themselves (from the 8th century BCE to 229 BCE when the Roman occupation began, the Greek city states battled each other and the Corfiots for control of the island), Byzantium, the Venetians,

---

[55] For those interested in such things, Hilary Whitton Paipeti's *In the Footsteps of Lawrence Durrell and Gerald Durrell in Corfu. A Modern Guidebook* (1998), provides several walks to look at the buildings, but see also the biographies mentioned above.

the Ottoman Empire, the French (1807-1814), the British (1815-1864), and the Italians and Germans during World War II (1941-1944).

During the Roman occupation the Corfiots made the mistake of siding with Anthony in his war with Octavian: in 31 BCE the latter wrought such havoc to the island that it took two centuries to recover. After the sundering of the Roman Empire, Corfu came under the suzerainty of what became the Byzantine Empire, during the final years of which the island suffered a succession of attacks by various forces including the Venetians, under whom the Corfiots finally placed themselves. The Venetian occupation lasted 410 years despite the strong sieges of 1537 and 1716 by the Ottoman Turks, the latter defeated with the aid of the German general Matthias Schulenberg, whose Carrara marble statue stands before the entrance to the Old Fort.

Venetian rule ended in 1797, when Napoléon Bonaparte and a revolutionary French Army occupied Venice and abolished the Serene State and shortly thereafter occupied Corfu. Two years later the French signed a truce with the besieging Russo-Turkish forces, which had been supported by a majority of the Corfiots because the French insulted their patron saint Spiridon. The Russians allowed a form of self-government by setting up "The Septinsular State," made up of the seven main Ionian Islands. In 1807, the Treaty of Tilsit gave Corfu back to the French, who constructed the arcaded building mirroring the rue de Rivoli in Paris along the Liston at the edge of the esplanade. This time they remained there until Napoleon's empire came to a disastrous end in 1814 and the victors at the Congress of Vienna established the "United States of the Ionian Islands," under the "protection" of Great Britain. Fifty years later, in 1864, the British finally bowed to the increasingly violent public desire for union with Greece and the Ionian Islands have been Greek ever since, with the exception of the Italian-German occupation during World War II.

All of these cultures left pieces of themselves and their works on the island and these are especially visible in the main urban center known as Corfu Town. The details about these remnants are available in any good guidebook and do not have to be rehearsed here.

The International Lawrence Durrell Society (ILDS), a scholarly fan club whose members are mostly college and university teachers of literature, decided in 1990, the year Durrell died, that every other of its bi-annual conferences would be held in locales where he had lived and worked. The ILDS held the first of these in Avignon in 1992,[56] the

---

[56] While Durrell never lived in Avignon, he spent much time there when he lived in Provence for the last 33 years of his life some 30-40 kilometers to the west of the old city of the Popes. His last major work entitled *The Avignon Quintet* (*Monsieur: or The Prince of Darkness* [1974], *Livia: or Buried Alive* [1978], *Constance: or Solitary Practices*

second in Alexandria, Egypt in 1996,[57] and the third on Corfu in 2000.[58]

The ILDS organized a tight six-day academic schedule for its Corfu conference, but fortunately left sufficient time and space for poetry readings, a rollicking if incoherent performance of some songs from Durrell's unfinished musical, "Ulysses Come Back," a fall-about-laughing reading of a play in several voices called, "At the Café Millenium with Aldington, Durrell, Faulkner, Fitzgerald & Hemingway" by the Hemingway scholar, H. R. Stoneback, a stirring performance of "Karaghiozi and Alexander the Great" by Eugenio Spatharis and his Shadow Puppet Theater (more about which below), a raucous final night banquet, and several excursions including a bus trip to see but not enter each of the villas noted above, as well as a trip by caïque (a small engine-driven boat that can hold about 35-40 fairly closely packed people) from the old Corfu Town harbor to the White House in Kalami for lunch in the open-air restaurant that now abuts the house and the unveiling of a plaque noting that Durrell had lived there. The only

---

[1982], *Sebastian: or Ruling Passions* [1983], and *Quinx: or The Ripper's Tale* [1985]), prominently features the city and its environs, some imagined, some real.

[57] The years in Egypt, 1941-45, resulted in Durrell's most famous work, *The Alexandria Quartet* (*Justine* [1957], *Balthazar* [1958], *Mountolive* [1958], and *Clea* [1960]).

[58] In 2004 the conference was held on the Greek island of Rhodes where Durrell lived from 1945 to 1947 when the British ruled there in the aftermath of the war.

jarring note here is the fact that Durrell's name is misspelled on the plaque, an error not yet corrected in June 2004, the last time we visited the village. The most important post-facto result of the ILDS Corfu conference was the establishment of the Durrell School of Corfu. Originally this was the work of one man: Richard Pine, a strikingly intelligent Irishman with a penchant for vulgarities at the appropriate moment and a taste for the grape shared by a number of us.[59] By 2000, he had worked for many years in the Irish public broadcasting world while writing books on Lawrence Durrell, Oscar Wilde and the Irish playwright Brian Friel, and attending several ILDS conferences where he gave deeply-thought papers on various aspects of Durrell's oeuvre.[60] While attending the Corfu conference, late one afternoon as he sat under the trees across the street from the

---

[59]That certain characteristics can be inherited is proven by the event at the airport in San Diego several years ago when Pine and his quick, bright daughter, Emilie, then what is currently called an "early teenager," flew in to attend an ILDS conference. Faced with a dullard immigration official who carped about one thing or another relating to Pine's passport, Emilie said to this dolt, "But my father wrote a book about Lawrence Durrell!" This of course should immediately have led to the return of his stamped passport and a smiling, "Welcome to the United States, sir." Needless to say it did not: instead the official said, "That *Alexandria Quartet* was real boring!" Somehow one is pleased that the fellow not only had *heard* of the books, but had actually *read* them, at least one likes to *think* he did.

[60] His books include *Lawrence Durrell: The Mindscape* (1994, rev. ed. 2005), *The Dandy and the Herald: Manners, Mind and Morals from Brummell to Durrell* (1988), *The Diviner: The Art of Brian Friel* (1999) and *The Thief of Reason: Oscar Wilde and Modern Ireland* (1995).

Cavalieri Hotel at the southern end of the Spianada (Esplanade) sipping a glass of un-resinated cool white wine, an idea expanded and spread like a benign bacillus through his brain and exploded into an epiphany: a meeting place for adventurous and enquiring minds, where the line between faculty and students would not entirely disappear perhaps, but would be deliberately blurred beyond the simple college paradigm. He envisioned a community of scholars of all ages and educational backgrounds gathered together for a week or more to talk about literature, the culture of the Hellenic world, ecology, philosophy, translation, the post-colonial experience in nations such as India, and the works of the Durrell brothers. Recognized scholars in these fields would introduce and guide the discussions and various "faculty" members would lecture on their specialties or subjects that interested them, following which everyone would talk about the subjects.

Thus one man's infatuation with the island and his obsession with the idea of a school, something like that of Socrates', devoted to themes associated with the Durrell brothers operating on the island where they spent their formative years, plus his energy and ability to convince others of the importance and necessity of realizing his dream, made it a reality two years later. In June 2002, the DSC held its first two-week session, followed by a reduced offering in 2003 and a full session in 2004.

After a week in Paris, Lynn-Marie and I flew to Greece for the 2002 session. The wait at the new Athens airport for the flight to Corfu was of such duration that we thought we should have brought along sleeping bags and a tent. The fact that this was not the old Athens airport, but rather the new one constructed in time for the 2004 Olympic Games at minimally 50% above original cost estimates, did not mitigate the length of annoyed time we spent, but in the end the Olympic Airlines airplane did take off, late of course. It must be admitted that we have spent several pleasant hours on several occasions in the airport restaurant named Olives, situated cheek by jowl with the McDonald's but serving a rather different type of food.

Our hotel, the Bella Venezia, located appropriately enough fairly close to the café where Richard Pine conceived of the School, certainly did not mind our not being on time; the people of Corfu are similar in one way to the residents of Key West: they roll with the metaphoric punches with an ease others find either contemptible (lazy, smelly, dirty, totally inefficient, what am I doing here, etc.) or admirable (no heart attacks here, Mabel, these people certainly know how to relax and enjoy life, even if the place smells of drains). The one oddity the hotel evidenced was the size and placement of the windows in the rooms: very small, oblong and two meters above the floor, which means one cannot see the sea unless one climbs up on a chair, but the sky is normally many shades of blue even when it rains.

This tardiness did not, however, mean we would be late for dinner since the Corfiots do not even begin to think about the evening meal until almost morning. No doubt I exaggerate somewhat. Nonetheless we did not get to the restaurant until ten o'clock that evening, after rounding up several other Durrell School of Corfu faculty members and their partners. The Chrysomalis restaurant, on Nickiforou Theotoki Street, a short walk from the Spianada, alleged to have been one of the Durrell brothers' favorite eateries, until recently contained a refrigerated display case cooled by a system made by a firm named Melissa, which Durrellians immediately associated with the eponymous character in *The Alexandria Quartet* and thus understood without hesitation why Larry Durrell liked the place. Over the years we have eaten there many times because the fall-off-the-bone roast lamb with roasted potatoes is a satisfaction bordering on a revelation, and the tzaziki and Greek salads captured our taste buds forever.[61]

---

[61] Tzaziki is a peasant's dish of sour yogurt mixed with chopped cucumbers, chives, olive oil and much garlic eaten with bread or matzos as an accompaniment to the main course or as an hors d'oeuvre. Oddly enough the recipe for this extremely tasty item is missing from the usually reliable Elizabeth David's *Mediterranean Cooking* as it is

That first night in the summer heat of 2002, we sat at the tables on the edge of the narrow street of the pedestrian zone so all the passersby could take note of what we consumed with such relish and gusto, and so we could hear one of Corfu Town's three philharmonic orchestras practice in a second story room above the restaurant set aside for that purpose. The entire band never played a complete piece or played all together: they practiced snippets of the compositions that apparently the conductor thought needed work. One of the pieces they rehearsed sounded suspiciously like the theme song from the American Indiana Jones movies. The name "philharmonic" should not fool anyone into thinking this aggregation consists of large numbers of musicians playing the usual variety of instruments. No, there are several such "philharmonia" in villages throughout the island, sometimes consisting of four full-time and a couple of part-time players of varying talents making on a limited number of instruments a form of music, most of which sound like marching tunes. The Corfu Town philharmonics boast a larger number of players than those in the villages. These bands did not always exist; indeed they date

from most cookbooks except those devoted to the kitchens of Greece. The ubiquitous Greek salad consists of quartered tomatoes, cucumber and red onion slices, black olives and feta cheese splashed with olive oil and sprinkled with a mixture of oregano, thyme and parsley. No more, no less. The quality of this salad seriously depends on the quality of the tomatoes and feta.

only from the British "protectorate" of the island. At one point the British governor refused to allow the military bands to participate in religious events, such as the four annual marches carrying the mummy of St. Spiridon through the streets on the saint's day. Ever inventive, the Corfiots organized their own band and there are now some nineteen such "philharmonia" on the island. The standard of tuition and playing is at such a level that brass and wind musicians from the island are in much demand in mainland orchestras.

About halfway through the meal the heavens opened their portals and the rains came. Without a moment's hesitation the waiters, the owner and the rest of us picked up the tables, chairs, food and wine and moved them to the other side of the narrow street under the arcade where we continued to eat and drink with the same gusto and increasing volume. Somehow one cannot imagine this happening with such sangfroid anywhere else. What the apartment dwellers above us thought of the grace and speed with which the diners and their plates were moved remains guesswork, but the volume of joyful noise we made would indicate the direction of their thoughts. Fortunately we ended the evening fairly early.

In the following years many of the participants in the School's programs stayed at the Konstantinopoulis Hotel, a six story square building with a flat façade bereft of exterior decoration facing the Town's old harbor. The rooms are small, but most of them look out over the harbor and the mist-shrouded shore of Albania to the east. The breakfast is more than adequate in a room eclectically decorated with wall-hangings ranging from facsimiles of 19th century real estate documents to a garish painting of a half-nude young woman staring the onlooker in the eye, not quite Olympia but almost as provocative. Because the hotel sits on the lower end of a great curving street that serves as one of the main routes to the hinterlands and suburbs there is a certain amount of street noise to be taken into account if one stays there. From time to time as the dawn breaks over the Albanian mountains the scratchy sound of the first bars of the Greek national anthem is heard for a brief moment before suddenly stopping as if someone jerked the needle off the ancient acetate recording. No one was able to explain the source of this tribute to the sunrise and Greek national sentiments. At the other end of the day one is liable to hear motor scooters ratcheting down the swerve of the street, carrying their happily tipsy human cargoes to their suburban or village beds.

If one leans slightly out the front room window and looks to the right one sees across the blue expanse of water the small island, islet really, of Vidos, little more than a kilometer away (or ten minutes by caïque ferry) between Corfu and the Albanian coast. This is one of the School's field class destinations because of its odd history and good but primitive swimming beach. The islet is currently unoccupied except for snakes, sea birds and various forms of insect life, but this was not always the case. The remnants of the Serbian army, forced out of Albania by the Allies in 1916, camped here under execrable conditions until the war's end in late 1918. More than 10,000 died from malnutrition and diseases before the assistance rendered by the Corfiots and the Greek government helped to stabilize the sanitary situation. The Serbian government went about its business for the same period of time on Corfu itself. The current Republic of Serbia and Montenegro affords itself a consulate on Corfu, which contains a museum devoted to these military and civilian experiences at the end of the Great War.

During the next world war the Italians built a two-story edifice on Vidos to serve as their occupation army headquarters and the islet served as a camp for Greek resistance members unfortunate enough to be captured by the Italian and German occupiers (1941-1944). After the war, the Greeks used the facilities as a prison for juvenile offenders, the governor of which lived in the former Italian military headquarters.

These days, when the captain is not unduly under the weather and the weather itself is sufficiently moderate to allow relatively calm passage, a caïque takes visitors across the water to visit the island and the great ossuary the Yugoslav government constructed in 1936 to hold the bones of the known and unknown soldiers who died there. Many of those whose bones do not rest here were taken out to sea and buried in the "Blue Graveyard." The victims are also commemorated by a large stone cross erected in 1922 on the grounds above the ossuary and its landscaped terraces overlooking the bay.

Armed with plenty of bottled water, the School's faculty and students walk over the narrow stony paths that crisscross Vidos listening to David Ashcroft relate the various histories of the place. At the end of the tour, by now hot and sweaty, back at the dock waiting for the caïque to return them to civilization, several of the more dehydrated of the group wonder aloud why the park authorities had not been thoughtful enough to provide a facility for dispensing cold beer. Indeed, this grumble becomes something of a lugubrious mantra chanted at every opportunity with tired chuckles until the ferry finally arrives. On the whole, the group despaired of finding any cold refreshment aboard this rather dilapidated vessel. To general surprise and mild astonishment, the captain, not himself a man to turn down a cold drink on a hot day, has in fact stocked a large metal cooler with bottles of Stella beer and the ubiquitous Coca-Cola. A great sigh of relief rises above the blue Ionian Sea and ten minutes later when the ferry reaches the old harbor the only bottles left in the cooler are empty. It had indeed been a very hot day to be tramping about the wastes of Vidos.

One place to escape the summer midday heat and still remain out of doors is the British Cemetery, located at the southern edge of Corfu Town near the prison above the San Rocco Square. One comes upon a limestone arch filled with a forbidding iron barred gate through which one sees what appears to be a large flower garden set amongst a small forest of pine trees and shrubbery. On the left pillar supporting the arch is a small metal sign explaining in Greek and English that the premises are administered by the "Commonwealth War Graves," despite the fact, as one soon learns, that very many of the graves hold civilians. Beneath this plaque in stark iron letters are the words "The British," from which one's eye automatically traverses to the right to read on that pillar, "Cemetery" with a certain feeling of completion. The gate itself is only opened for hearses plying their trade; visitors enter by a smaller iron gated portal five or six meters further down the stone wall that encloses the grounds. As one pushes the gate open a small bell tingles loudly to inform the keepers that visitors have entered the precincts of the graveyard.

In fact, the pine-shaded grounds consist of the space devoted to various sizes of markers with widely divergent bits of information and theological texts adorning the stones, and the well-maintained gardens through which wind narrow but discernable pathways. In full summer bloom the boisterous flowers add a minor riot of color to the otherwise gray-beige-brown of the funerary section and the grounds are carpeted with great swaths of wild orchids. A company of turtles, cats and other creatures small and beautiful, multi-colored butterflies and plain black flies, ants and insects of unknown origin move lethargically through the hot air or simply lie in the sun, peaceful and tranquil as the atmosphere itself.

The British have been here since the Napoleonic Wars and the creation of the United States of the Ionian Islands under British "protection" arranged at the Congress of Vienna in 1815. They continue to bury their dead in this sanctuary of quietude. One of the more recent deceased is the Australian actor-teacher-writer, Kester Berwick (1903-1992).[62] What might come as a surprise to the visitor is the large number of graves containing German sailors, most of who perished before and during the First World War. There seems to be no explanation as to why members of the enemy naval forces are buried in

---

[62] See the aforementioned *Corfu. A Novel* by Robert Dessaix in which Berwick is a featured, if absent, player.

what is essentially a civilian cemetery. The British military is represented by a mass grave containing 44 bodies of sailors, victims of what is known as The Corfu Incident of 1946.[63] A dispute between the British and Albanian governments on the question of whether or not the channel between Corfu and the Albanian coast was to be considered international waters, as the British insisted, or Albanian waters, as the Albanians insisted, led to the Albanians firing on two British cruisers on May 14, 1946. The Albanians missed the ships but annoyed the British whose ships were engaged in clearing mines placed in the channel by the Germans during the war. An exchange of bitter diplomatic notes led to no solution and on October 22 four British warships entered the channel with orders to return fire if fired upon. This turned out to be unnecessary. Two of the ships struck mines and limped into the Corfu harbor attended by the other two. Forty-four men were killed and another 40 wounded; one of the ships had to be scrapped. Investigation showed the mines were new and had been put in place recently. The British government sued the Albanians in the International Court and won damages the Albanians refused to pay. The British navy buried its dead in the Corfu British cemetery amidst the orchids, towering pines and sweet quietude.

---

[63] Not to be confused with The Corfu Incident of 1923, which is quite a different matter.

In a society that thrives on noise, peace and quiet are valuable commodities and should be cherished. Thus far the Durrell School has not held a class in this spot, but it is not impossible that one day it will offer a guided tour of the grounds.

One can eat very well, simply, and healthily on Corfu, but it is good to keep certain things in mind when choosing the components of one's meals. One night in 2003, we sat at an outside table at a restaurant in the center of Corfu Town wanting to eat fish. As in many Greek eateries, the waiter invited us to go into the kitchen to look over the fresh fish and to choose a couple for our dinner. All very well and good, but we neglected to ask the cost and had momentarily forgotten that fresh fish on Corfu is a rare delicacy the price of which reflects this rarity. Since the waters in the Ionian Sea are largely fished out, fresh fish is imported at great cost, which of course is passed on to the consumer. The cook prepared the fish to perfection, it's true, but the bill at the end of the dinner came as an unpleasant surprise. It should not have, of course, but it did. This is a shame since fresh grilled fish there is one of the wonders of the culinary universe, and indeed with some effort, or the help of friends who live on the island, in this case the Ashcrofts, one can find fresh fish in restaurants, but outside Corfu Town. For example, we ate fine grilled fish at a restaurant called Klimateria (grape vine) in a seashore town Benitses and at one called Voularis, the two neatly bracketing the city to the south and the north respectively.

Indeed, we have always eaten very well, if not exquisitely, on Corfu. It may be possible to eat an exquisite meal (meaning the equivalent of a one-star in the Michelin red guide) on the island, but this outing will put a considerable dent in one's bank account. And why bother, when for less money one can consistently eat wildly flavored meals in comfortable restaurants at their summer out door tables? One night I drank the best house red wine I've ever tasted bar none at a small taverna called the Moraghia, just before the old harbor overlooking the sea with the Albanian coast in the distance. The consensus at the table was that she shouldn't, but Susan MacNiven ordered grilled octopus and I must say I was impressed. Not as much as she, though: Susan ordered it the next three times she and Ian ate there! Here, too, we have returned many times and on our first night there in June 2004, the waiters smiled and greeted us with the words, "Grilled lemon chicken!" We had eaten this dish several times the previous year. It is nice to be remembered.

A word about the local wines is in order here. Normally one is rather skeptical of wine served in carafes in less than one-star restaurants. In many but certainly not all of the eateries on Corfu, especially those in Corfu Town, drinking the carafe wine is recommended, particularly for those whose appreciation of the grape results in copious consumption of the vineyard's product. There are two reasons for this: cost and next-day comfort. The carafe wines are usually less expensive than the bottled variety and can be as drinkable as most of those varieties. And, since the local wines meant for local consumption are not saturated with preservative chemicals, one's hangover the following day is considerably meliorated. This, one supposes, is also a form of paradise. This is not to say there isn't a time and place for bottled wine; there certainly is, but one should usually order bottles at the higher-priced restaurants when one is splurging anyway. In tavernas, the best advice is to stick to the local plonk.

In the School's brief history, its programs followed a general pattern: The first two days are devoted to a symposium on a specific topic such as "Globalization and Nationalism," and "Understanding Misunderstanding," the latter of which dealt with how cultures misunderstand each other, a theme chosen in part as a result of the terrorist attacks in New York and Washington, and the rise of terrorism generally. (The 2003 session did not offer a symposium because the lack of registrants, due to fears of travel, caused the School to hold only a five day "rump" session, deferring the planned symposium and seminars until 2004.) The following two weeks are taken up with seminars, lectures and field classes.

In 2002, all the first week's lectures were of considerable interest to the auditors and two of them were outstanding: David Bellamy's and mine. I say this with no false sense of modesty because I am a good lecturer, a touch melodramatic perhaps, but audience members rarely fall asleep during my presentations. David's style is much more physical and he knows his subject so well that he only needs a few notes to guide him. He is so wrapped up in his theme that he sometimes jumps up and down: Think of this large, burly, white-haired and bearded 73-year-old botanist, terribly articulate if occasionally in his enthusiasm incomprehensibly Oxbridge in accent, dressed in an old polo shirt, shorts, and sandals, lifting himself dramatically off the floor to make a point about how endangered species of flora and fauna *can* be saved, how dried wetlands *can* be reinvigorated, how entire dying regions around the world *can* be brought back to life, and giving examples of places where he has successfully worked to do this, in a presentation both witty and learnèd. He is appropriately a star on BBC-TV and in many documentary films about his work.

To go on a walk in the countryside with him in the group is to return hours later than envisioned by the schedule: every other meter he stops to examine a plant or a nest or a tree, and tells you its history, where it grows differently, why it is dying (over spraying with chemicals to ensure the grape harvest is plentiful), and so on. At one point he took off his sandals and leapt into an irrigation ditch by the path to call attention to some water plant he'd not previously encountered on Corfu or that part of the world. This occurred on a long walking tour through the now legendary "chessboard fields," so named by the young Gerald Durrell in the 1930s when he examined the wildlife in the area with his mentor, the radiologist and naturalist, Dr. Theodore Stephanides.[64]

A rare man Bellamy is, and it is a rare privilege to be with him. He also does not refuse a touch of

---

[64] Stephanides (1896-1983) met the Durrell family soon after their arrival on Corfu and remained a close friend of the entire family, but especially Larry and Gerry, for the rest of his life. He appears in the books both brothers wrote about Corfu and in Henry Miller's *The Colossus of Maroussi* (1941). Larry dedicated *The Greek Islands* (1979) and Gerry *Birds, Beasts & Relatives* (1969) and *The Amateur Naturalist*, written with Lee Durrell, to their old friend. Among his many scientific and popular publications, his memoir of prewar life on the Greek islands and the Durrell family, *Island Trails* (1973 with an introduction by Gerry), and *Climax in Crete* (1946) about his military experiences in 1941 on that island are of particular interest for the general reader.

the grape himself and tells wonderful stories, some pungent but always both amusing and edifying. Walking with him in 2004 over the hills of northern Corfu around the village of Perithia was an experience equal to that of two years earlier, except there was no ditch into which he could leap. His enthusiasm and willingness to answer any question make him a wonderful teacher and guide. He has published over thirty books and his autobiography is appropriately titled, *Jolly Green Giant* (2002).[65] He inscribed a copy of the book for the Durrell School library, "For the most important library I know." A generous man in addition to his other attributes.

(I should add in fairness that we were unable to remain on Corfu for the second week of the School's first year's sessions, so were not able to attend the other lectures and seminars. Therefore, it is entirely possible that one or two of the second week's lectures might have reached the level of mine, but they are unlikely to have achieved the heights of David Bellamy's.)

The faculty in the last three years has boasted many excellent lecturers and scholars, several of whom are very well known in their fields, such as Gayatri Chakravorty Spivak, the literary

---

[65] Unfortunately, this lively, learned and amusing book is not published in the USA, but it is readily available from one or another of the bookselling web sites in that country.

critic/historian from Columbia University;[66] Terry Eagleton, the former proponent of what is known in academia as Critical Theory who now doubts the usefulness of these tenets but who holds on to his mildly Marxist beliefs;[67] Harish Trivedi, the professor of literature at the University of Delhi, known for his work on the theoretical and practical bases of translation in its broadest cultural sense, whose sense of humor belies but does not negate his reputation as a severely critical thinker;[68] Lee Durrell, the zoologist who actively continues her late husband's work through the Durrell Wildlife Conservation Trust on the island of Jersey; Ian MacNiven, a leading Durrellian with a wicked wit; Elemer Hankiss of the Hungarian Academy of Sciences; John Brandon of the Asia Foundation in Washington DC; Nicholas Gage, the former New York Times investigative journalist and author of many books including *Eleni* (1983), in which he describes his investigation into his mother's murder during the Greek Civil war; Anthony Hirst,

---

[66]Her publications include *In Other Worlds: Essays in Cultural Politics* (1988), *Don't Call Me Postcolonial: From Kant to Kwakubo* (1998) and *A Critique of Postcolonial Reason* (1999).

[67]*Literary Theory: An Introduction* (1987), *Scholars and Rebels in 19ᵗʰ Century Ireland* (1999), *After Theory* (2003), and *Sweet Violence* (2003).

[68]*Colonial Transactions: English Literature and India* (1995); and as editor (with Richard Allen), *Literature and Nation: Britain and India 1800-1990* (2001), (with Susan Bassnett) *Postcolonial Translation: Theory and Practice* (1998) and (with Meenakshi Mukherjee) *Interrogating Postcolonialism: Theory, Text and Context* (1996).

a Postdoctoral Research Fellow in Byzantine and Modern Greek Literature at Queen's University in Belfast who is editing a critical edition of Cavafy's published poems;[69] Gerald Dawe, a poet and teacher at Trinity College Dublin, whose published poetry collections include *The Morning Train* (1999) and *Lake Geneva* (2003); Eve Patten, a lecturer in English at Trinity College Dublin, who has also lectured at the University of Bucharest and is, logically enough, writing a critical study of Olivia Manning's novels;[70] James Nichols, emeritus professor of English, author of the novel *Children of the Sea* (1977) and many essays and articles on Durrellian subjects, currently finishing a study of the women in Lawrence Durrell's fiction, which promises to be quite controversial; and Maria Misra, a lively lecturer and fellow of Keble College at Oxford University and author of *Business, Race and Politics in British India* (1999) and the forthcoming *History of India since the Mutiny* (2005).

---

[69] He most recently co-edited with Michael Silk the book, *Alexandria, Real and Imagined* (2004), the essays in which deal with the entire spectrum of Alexandrian history and include two on Durrell's *Alexandria Quartet*.

[70] Manning's husband taught English in Bucharest in 1940 when the German presence in the city took on alarming proportions and the local anti-Semitic fascists spread terror through the streets. They ended up spending the war in Cairo having followed a similar escape route taken by the Durrells and others: Athens, Crete, Alexandria, and, finally, Cairo. Manning used the experience to write *The Balkan Trilogy* and *The Levant Trilogy*, filmed by BBC-TV as a mini-series in 1987 called *Fortunes of War*.

Others who have taught at the School are perhaps not yet as well known or published as the examples above, and indeed have included non-academics such as Nuala ni Dhomhnaill (pronounced NOO-la Nee GO-nal), the well-known Irish poet who writes in the Irish language, whose published work available in English includes *Pharoah's Daughter* (1990), *The Astrakhan Cloak* (1992) and *The Water Horse* (1999); and graduate Ph.D. students such as James Gifford (University of Alberta), Beatrice Skordili (Syracuse University) and Isabelle Keller (University of Toulouse le Mirail), each of whom has published essays on various aspects of the Durrell oeuvre. It is in fact in part the inclusion of these bright younger scholars that gives the School its unique character as a community of interested, knowledgeable, and mentally adventurous minds interacting with one another.

Indeed, the international nature of the students and faculty lends itself to discussions over a wide range of subjects to which each brings a national point of view to liven the mix. Participants in the seminars and lectures have come from Ireland (two of them sponsored by Trinity College, Dublin), Greece, Australia, India, the USA, England, Hungary (including two students sponsored by grants from the Hellenic Bottling Company), Switzerland, France, Taiwan, the Netherlands,

Canada, and the Conch Republic.[71] The formal education levels vary widely and their professions also veer from the academic (university and high-school teachers, administrators) through the business world (executives and accountants), playwrights and theater managers, foundation/research center scholars and administrators, poets, journalists, zoo directors, botanists, novelists and ethnographers to graduate students in several disciplines.

"Dave, Bill, and the students save Bruno from drowning." This could be the title of one of the more dramatic events that occurred during the first year of the School's existence. "Bruno" being what I was called by the children of my acquaintance in Heidelberg in the early 1960s who couldn't get their untrained tongues around "Brewster." The reference to the Renoir film is of

---

[71] The Conch Republic consists of the land encompassed by the legal geographic limits of the city of Key West, constituted in 1982 as result of various Federal Government agencies shutting down the single highway up the keys to the mainland in a surprise blockade to sniff out and capture drug dealers, in the process crippling the flow of tourists which are the city's economical life-blood. The mayor and the city council, supported by an apparent majority of the population, seceded from the Union and formed the independent Conch Republic, the Secretary General of which continues to issue passports and other formal documents. The Republic also boasts its own flag, which flies throughout the island on houses of the locally patriotic citizens.

course deliberate, though the plot's dénouement is quite different. It all began in the summer of 2000 during the Durrell conference on Corfu.

As noted above, in *Prospero's Cell* (1945) there is a brief paragraph about the shrine of Saint Arsenius, the protector of fishermen, sailors and their enterprises, located on the rocks of a small cove accessible only by water to which Durrell and his friends brought oil for the lamp and swam in the crystalline water, his wife Nancy diving for cherries they tossed into the sea (diary entry 18.5.37). The writer returns to the shrine in the essay "Oil for the Saint; Return to Corfu," reprinted in *Spirit of Place* (1969), in which he writes, "So long as Saint Arsenius is there the Greek world will remain right side up." At least the first part of the thought is true: the saint is still there.

Because the cove is only a couple of headlands from Kalami, a village on the northeastern coast of the island where the White House, in which Nancy and Lawrence lived for several years, sits on the edge of the water in the harbor, it has become a place of pilgrimage for readers who then sail on to the restaurant next to the White House for lunch on the terrace. This was the chronology of events in 2000 when two boatloads of Durrellians motored to the cove in caïques, pronounced "kai-eekay," and many plunged into the clear water diving for cherries tossed by those who remained aboard the small motor boats. The fact that I remained on board bothered me since then: though I cannot swim more than a couple of meters before sinking inexorably to the bottom, I should have made the attempt. Or so I thought.

The chronology during the 2002 School session somehow got reversed and the caïque dropped us off at the makeshift dock below the White House for lunch before we visited the cove and the shrine. This is important to remember when contemplating what followed. The lunch began with the usual bread and butter, pitchers of red and white wine already chilled on the tables as the 25 or 30 of us clamored into seats and raised a glass to the beautiful sunny day and Durrell's good fortune to have lived here before mass tourism blighted the island. The menu at the restaurant is simple and straight-forward: tzazikis goes with the bread, followed by the first course of eel cooked in a red sauce that will knock your socks off with bursts of flavors should you be wearing socks, an improbable piece of clothing for the island in the summer. The second course consists of whatever fish is available served grilled with the Greek equivalent of Provençal herbs and lemon and a form of ratatouille. Should fish not be available, the ubiquitous roast lamb that actually tastes like lamb is a satisfactory substitute, unless one doesn't like the taste of lamb, and in this highly unlikely event one can order chicken or a vegetarian dish.

The wine does not stop flowing unless one insists. There is a dessert but I cannot recall what it could have been.

I sat with three bright and attractive students from Denison University and their literature teacher, our friend Professor Dr. Richard Hood, also known as one half of the touring Bristol Brothers Appalachian music group. The students and I joined our efforts to help Richard prepare his lecture on the rather arcane subject of cabalistic mysticism, mystery cults and modernity and a grand time was had by all, especially by me. Fortunately I had given my lecture earlier that morning.

The time arrived for our departure and we all trooped back down the pier to the caïque and piled aboard. Several chugging minutes later we entered the cove and there stood the shrine, the size of a telephone booth halfway up the low shoreline of rocks, the same as it had been in the 1930s. No cherries this year, but several adventurous folk leapt into the water and swam to the shore and climbed up to see if the door to the shrine could be easily opened. It could not, but this was actually irrelevant. You have probably guessed what happened next. It is true.

Rashly, spurred on by the frustration of not having done so the last time, rowelled by the no doubt excessive amount of wine consumed with lunch, I stripped out of my clothes, partially and inadequately hidden by a towel held by my long suffering beloved Lynn-Marie, yanked on my swim trunks and leapt into the sea to the assorted shouts of encouragement and dismay of my fellow pilgrims. Having swallowed a half-liter of salt water and righted myself in the water, I began to thrash my way toward the shore like a demented white whale. A couple of the students swam along at my sides in case I sank like a stone, or one stoned. Finally, after what seemed like an hour but was more likely a minute, I grasped the rocks and dragged my heaving body up where I lay gasping like a half-dead fish too long out of water.

Regaining my regular breathing rhythm, if not my sanity, I crawled up the rocks to the shrine and peered into it through a hole in the door, seeing nothing in the darkness, but imagining the saucer with olive oil and a primitive wick waiting to be lit by another pilgrim who had the keys to the kingdom, or at least the door.

The captain jerked the boat's hooting mechanism to call us back to the caïque. He had a schedule, after all, and was paid to keep to it. Balancing precariously on the last rock on my bare feet, somewhat sobered by the swim from the boat, I contemplated the madness of what I was about to do. But there was nothing for it and I once again leapt into the breech, so to say, and flopped about in the general direction of the waiting boat, surrounded by all three Denison students and the semi-professional swimmers David Ashcroft and William Godshalk shouting encouragements but also for the last several meters holding me up and moving me forward. Without their help I surely would have drowned. Back on the boat I vowed to learn how to swim sufficiently well to make that short trip again next year. Ah, well, the best laid plans of mice and men, yes.

The evening meal that night tasted particularly scrumptious and I savored every morsel. And the wine had a special, Greek tang on the tongue. To my saviors I say a hearty and deeply felt, Ἐυχαριστω![72]

The following year the participants in the School's rump session who took the excursion lived through what can honestly be described as an extraordinary experience. The seminar topic for this field class, led by Richard Pine, was to have been "Writing Against the Grain" with Durrell's *The Black Book* (1939) as the basis for discussion. The use of the conditional in the sentence above indicates that there are occasionally forces of nature against which humans have not as yet developed antidotes. As the caïque moved off

---

[72] David and Alexina Ashcroft live for most of the year in a Venetian manor house they are renovating in a village at the northern end of Corfu. Alex is the Durrell School of Corfu's administrative director and Dave guides many of the School's field classes and walks throughout Corfu Town and venues all over the island. William Godshalk is a professor of literature at the University of Cincinnati (Ohio) who has written and lectured widely on modern English-language literature with an emphasis on Durrell's works.

from the quay in the old harbor the sky threatened but held back, as if waiting to see in which direction the group would sail. The captain of the boat did not seem unduly worried and the mate did not concern himself with the weather, taking great care that his silver reflecting sunglasses sat properly on his sun-browned nose. Saint Spiridon and Saint Arsenius must have been busy elsewhere.

As the caïque rounded the headland it became clear once again how over-development has wrecked the beauty and simplicity of the shoreline and the hills above the bay. The only remnant of the time Larry and Nancy lived there is the White House itself, now an expensive rental villa. Just as the boat neared the primitive cement dock at the White House, a rainstorm began to pelt the water in small but extensive explosions. The staff of the restaurant hurriedly began to attach large sheets of plastic to the open sides of the terrace, and the captain of the caïque with great gusto leapt boldly into the bay, swimming about with the grace of a sea lion at home in these waters. After all, he seemed to tell the group, what is a little rainwater? One might have agreed with him until the raindrops turned into hailstones the size of marbles and increased in number and intensity, in addition to which the temperature dropped precariously, causing a great wave of shivering to overtake the drenched scholars. These wrapped themselves in towels and other pieces of textile meant to keep them dry, and scurried off the boat into the relative shelter of the restaurant, the tables of which were fortunately already stocked with bread, olive oil and carafes of red and white wine.

There is a theory in the restaurant industry, which recommends that no matter what the conditions on any given day, usually related to the tardiness of serving the meal and the consequent growling and discomfort of the customers, immediately serve drinks and something to nibble on, be it ever so simple as chunks of fresh bread and good olive oil for dipping. The White House restaurant staff may never have heard of this theory qua theory, but experience surely told them this was the way to go about taking care of the clientele.

The seminar on writing against the grain, however, could not compete with the hail and rain pounding and rattling on the tin roof and generally raising hell with the customers and the staff, the latter of whom performed their jobs with magnificent aplomb in the face of unexpected adverse inclement weather, which was certainly against the grain of what one could normally expect there and then. The restaurant's owner assured everyone that nothing like this had occurred in the last 20 or so years. The School's participants agreed that it was a fitting moment, given the nature of the day's subject matter. Larry

Durrell would no doubt have smiled and ordered another glass of wine, allowing as how it was fitting for the island Shakespeare had in mind for *The Tempest*.

And so several of those under the tin roof enjoying the varied courses that appeared as if by magic, also raised their wine-drenched tumblers. Alas, the tempest also threw off the schedule sufficiently so that the captain suggested in no uncertain terms that a stop at the shrine of Saint Arsenius to genuflect and swim, as the Durrells had done in the 1930s, would not fit his notion of the time he should be back at the old harbor of Corfu Town, and thus this, as the discussion of writing against the grain, had to be postponed until the School's 2004 summer session. The White House restaurant owner assured the DSC that no tempests would disrupt the field class to his place next year, calling on Saint Arsenius to be his witness and protector of his statement.

As it turned out, the restaurateur was prescient. The weather in 2004 was perfect for the jaunt, the food tasted the same, the wine flowed from small carafes and laughter danced among the tables on the terrace. Richard Pine spoke a few words in front of the Durrell plaque before lunch and quoted a line or two from the works as the group gathered around him in the street, parting from time to time to allow curious villagers and tourists to pass through wondering what could have caused this gathering of non-Greeks carrying books, of all things, and vaguely attentive looks on their faces. The stop at the Saint Arsenius shrine allowed those who could swim to do so; these included Lynn-Marie for the first time in addition to the wonder dog, Pip, the Ashcrofts' small white and brown Jack Russell who simply jumped off the boat into the water with no hesitation and swam ashore where he indulged his doggy proclivities before returning to the caïque, not forgetting to shake himself dry as soon as he again stood among the passengers. Pip quickly became the School's mascot and attended most of the social events to everyone's delight.

Animals do not normally play a role in the proceedings of the Durrell School of Corfu, but there are two exceptions: Pip of course and the animals attended to by Sylvia Dimitriadis Steen and her Silva Project. Located on the vast family estate on a hill to the south of Corfu Town, Mrs. Steen is devoting her life to saving the Skyrian ponies from extinction.

This small mountain horse, similar in size to the Lilliputian ponies in Vienna, existed for centuries as the driving force behind the wheat threshers and other farming equipment, particularly on the island of Skyros. Like farmers throughout the planet, Greek peasants can be very attentive to, and caring for, their animals; they can also be callously indifferent to their fate when no longer needed as labor. In the 1960s, when mechanized equipment finally made its way to the islands, the ponies' usefulness declined and the farmers neglected them. European Union support for farms raising sheep and goats means the ponies' grazing lands are being decimated by the other animals. The situation was complicated by a Skyros law forbidding purebred ponies from being exported, which meant that the peasants mated the ponies with donkeys so the resulting mules could be sold off the island. In 1998, of the 158 ponies remaining on the island only 30 were purebreds. Years ago the University of Thessalonika was able to obtain several of the latter for study purposes and in 1996 Mrs. Steen was asked to provide shelter for their descendents. This small woman with a large heart and a vast supply of energy decided to prevent the extinction of these beautiful animals and thus the Silva Project was born.

Mrs. Steen has generously welcomed each year's School participants to her estate for a tour of the landscape (including the gorgeous panorama of the island's eastern shoreline), a talk about the history of the Project animated by her deep enthusiasm, and a grand banquet on the broad terrace abutting the main house. When Mrs. Steen greeted visitors at the door, she was usually accompanied by a sheep that lived in the house with the dogs and cats, that seriously believed Mrs. Steen to be its mother, and followed her everywhere. Unfortunately the sheep died during the winter of 2003-04 as Mrs. Steen began a process to convince it that it was in fact an animal and should sleep outside with the others of its kind. Perhaps the sheep could not face the possibility of being alienated from its putative maternal parent.

The annual visit to the Silva Estate is one of the highlights of the School's summer session, not only because the food and drink are copious and excellent, but also because it allows the participants to mingle with the Estates' volunteer staff in a beautiful setting and do what intellectuals do: talk.

Several other field classes have been repeated over the years because they take advantage of local cultural and historical sites. On the mainland, the School's participants travel by ferry and bus to the village of Lia tucked into a mountain range. This is the birthplace of Nicholas Gage, the Greek-American author and journalist whose book, *Eleni* (1983), tells with great passion and insight the story of his mother's politically motivated murder in the village during the terrible years of the Greek civil war (1944-1949). Gage himself has on several occasions guided the participants through the history of the village and its fate, exemplary of so many villages and towns in which both fanatical conservatives and communists lived and killed each other. The author has supported the reconstruction of his family's house and the construction of an inn with a restaurant and a dozen rooms to help the village to stabilize its economic base.

Somewhat further afield, the School organizes a one-day excursion by boat to the Albanian coast to visit the archeological site at Butrint, now a UNESCO World Heritage site. This is made somewhat easier by recent political changes in that country and offers the opportunity to learn about the various layers of Greek, Roman, Byzantine and Turkish cultures in this part of the Mediterranean basin. The site dates back to the 8th century BCE and was also at various times under Corfiot and Venetian rule, and contains a baptistery and basilica from the 6th century CE.

Back on Corfu itself, the Ionian Cultural Museum in Sinarades, situated in an ancient two-story farmhouse, contains artifacts relating to the economic history of the island, especially its agricultural basis, and oddly enough, documents on the rescue of British and American fliers shot down by the Germans during World War II. And a visit to the old Angevin castle ruins on a hill in the seaside town of Kassiopi on Corfu's northeastern edge allowed David Ashcroft to expound about the medieval period of the island's history. The castle ruins also afford the visitor a magnificent view of the Ionian Sea, a sight far more pleasing to the eye than the overdeveloped tourist center that the town of Kassiopi has become.

Leaving the town the participants travel by bus to a small village in the mountains to tour a Venetian manor house and learn about the long Venetian occupation of the island during the height of the Venice Republic's power. The lovely view out over the valley at sunset adds a non-academic aspect to the end of the day, saluted with a rough young red wine made by the owners of the manor house and served with a fine assortment of Greek hors d'oeurves. The Ashcrofts know a thing or two about hospitality, in addition to their vast knowledge of Corfu's long history.

There is always something new to discover in places one returns to, and Corfu is no exception. For example, the Archeological Service and the Museum of Asian Art housed in the Palace of St. Michael and St. George. Founded in 1927 by the diplomat Gregorios Manos with a donation of 10,500 pieces of Chinese and Japanese art, this is the only one of its kind in Greece. After 1974, additional collections from central Asia expanded the institution into a general Asian museum. As for the Palace itself, the British built the neo-classical edifice in Maltese stone starting in 1819 as the residence of its Lord High Commissioner, meant to be the most splendid building on the island as befits the most powerful "protector" of the Ionian Islands. At the same time the Knights of the Order of St. Michael and St. George also established their headquarters in the building, thus its present name. Established in 1818, the Order served as a support group for British officials in service in the Ionian Islands and Malta, a sort of elite fraternal organization. In 1864, when the British relinquished their power, the Palace passed into the hands of the Greek state.

At the south end of the building there is an Art Café with a fine garden overlooking the sea abutting the Municipal Gallery and a small exhibition space that seems to have nothing to do with the Gallery. Such relationships on the island are often murky to outsiders, and many locals as well. One summer, the exhibition space held photographs of Cuba and Guatemala taken by a local photographer on a grant; not bad, but not exceptional. The Gallery is housed in a large section of the Palace, where portraits of local gentry and gentle images of the island's landscapes dominate the collection and there are a few abstract pieces that the curator no doubt somehow snuck past the board of directors when the members dozed off during a long meeting or two.

The Durrell School has held seminars in the Café's garden and in the banquet room of the Municipal Gallery, always careful in the latter venue to finish on time so the guard would not be discommoded by the necessity of knocking on the door to announce something along the lines of, "Hurry up, please, it's time," in Greek of course. Seminars and lectures have also been given in the grand old building that houses the Corfu Reading Society at the north eastern high end of Kapodistriou Street and in the Ionian Cultural Centre, the latter beautifully situated on the water at the Faliraki peninsula on the water below the Reading Society. Unfortunately, the manager of the Cultural Centre managed to over-schedule the facilities for June 2004, squeezing the School out of its contract to use the facilities, leading to some swift juggling of schedule and venues, ably handled by Alexina Ashcroft, the School's administrative director.

Established in 1836 by liberals influenced by the revolutionary movements spreading throughout Europe at the time, the Corfu Reading Society is the oldest cultural institution in modern Greece. Originally organized to purchase literature and journals from western Europe, the Society quickly became the meeting place for the cultured elite on the island, who gradually turned it into a center propagating the notion of the union of the United States of the Ionian Islands with the Greek state. Its collections contain a specialized library of approximately 7000 volumes on the Ionian Islands and a general library of about 50,000 volumes that can be consulted by scholars and other researchers. The rooms are richly appointed and serve as reading-study centers in addition to meeting and reception spaces. From time to time the School holds its seminars in the Society's facilities.

The Durrell School is no exception to the rule that external changes necessitate internal modifications. Given the current (late 2004) hesitation for many to travel beyond the confines of their own countries, the increasing complexities of organizing a complicated but top quality learning and teaching forum on a fairly isolated island, and the fluctuating value of major western currencies, the School's directors decided in 2004 that in the future they will annually offer two or three week-long seminars devoted to a single subject (for example, genius and madness) rather than a single two-week session devoted to several different topics. How this will play out remains to be seen. What is clear from past experience, however, is the fact that Richard Pine's original vision of a community of scholars from various backgrounds, ages and education levels can, with sufficient effort, funds and expenditure of time, be satisfactorily, often transcendentally realized. This is a large accomplishment, to which the glories of Corfu add the splendid setting for the experiment to take place.

III. METAFICTIONS

Portaria

(For Wolfgang and Ute Benz)

One night in the summer
    We drove to the village above the harbor
Where cottages hang on the mountainside –
    Pools of light in the deep black sky,
Cars crouched silently in the streets –
    Chariots of our time awaiting centurions,
Careful goats freely roam the lanes –
    Memories of bloody sacrifice.

Tourists at heart we step cautiously
    On paths where schoolbook figures
Wore out their cranky leather sandals
    Discussing the star's comforting behavior.
There are no analogies today and
    Our symbols, too, repeat theirs,
No burden is too light for them to bear;
    Classic references no longer suffice.

Alone on the paths in our own present
    We have no recourse to literature;
We drink new wine, bemused, nostalgic,
    While freighters come and go
In the darkened harbor far below
    Silently winking at us through the night.

(1980)

At the Edge: The Tune Inn

The Tune Inn's raucous chili
seasoned with Waylon's whiskey growl
bites memory's taste buds
here among the olive trees and lemons
and the melodic cries of "ça va?"

No one here yells "86 the bum!"
Here where waiters practice the ultimate snub
you become an unperson, Mamie,
let me tell you they know the tricks!
Desperadoes all of them, uncouth.
When they rush to ask, "Vous choisi?"
I reach for the aspirin in my bag, let me tell you.

There are no signs here for Burma Shave.

(Tavel, October 1983)

222

Sitges Afternoon

IN THE EARLY SPRING when it rains on the east coast of Spain the drops fall softly. The surf modulates the sound of the rain in the street and on our balcony. Or so we thought. What we could not understand were the bright mornings full of enough sun to burn our skin and last through a late lunch on the balcony above the beach – then the swift change in the afternoon when clouds blotted out the sun, chilling the air, and the rain started as soft as it was sudden. This was the time for cognac and reading and sleeping. Occasionally I tried to write a paragraph, but rarely succeeded so quit trying to make something else out of immediate sensations.

Later, ignoring the loud sports broadcast from the next room in the hotel, came the time for gentle awakening and loving quietly, as soft as the rain outside in the early evening Spanish light.

Sometimes I thought she had vaguely awakened and wanted to touch me, but noticed I was writing. Not wanting to disturb, me she drifted silently back into a shallow sleep.

And what was I doing then? Dreaming of the Mediterranean while looking at its slow blueness?

Remembering her salty skin, or cognac bursting in the back of my throat, or a mind disjointed by sexual longing, or even the simple joy of being sunburned?

The disparate afternoon gave way to the evening and thoughts of food and walking the glistening narrow lanes of the seashore town. By then it would not matter if it rained, however softly.

(1980)

Searching for Color

IT HAD BEEN A GRAND EXPERIMENT, but it did not last: watercolors do not poison but seep into the paper in waving lines. What they needed in that foreign landscape proved to be straight lines leading directly to the fires of Saint Elmo's domain. Too far inland, only fatty growths on their wrists flourished. Their soles toughened and cracked under the weight of constant sun and the grainy paths they trod so eagerly in their search for the myth's end. The myth, of course, was as endless as a circle, but they had no way of knowing this when they started; no one told them and they did not know to ask.

Soon the hysteria of the local dogs began to erode the stability of their commitment and the villagers began to shake their heads at the increasingly odd behavior of these strangers. The opera could not contain the volume of their passion: the soprano left for home muttering to her keeper, and the baritone leaped from a small privately-owned airplane over the square on which the opera house stood.

No one admired their perseverance in continuing the search, because no one realized they were searching: no one had asked and they had volunteered nothing but their affable smiles and ability to learn the language at a reasonable rate of speed and comprehension. They began to cruise in an ever-diminishing radius and then refused to leave the yellow garden smelling of onions and rosemary. More and more they lost their contours and personal colors, until one day, passersby could no longer distinguish them from anything else in the yellow garden, so well had they blended with the environment. In this way, perhaps, they had found what they sought. They were, after all, human like you and me.

(1986)

Success and Failure

TWENTY-FIVE TIMES we tried to climb the face of the mountain and each time we failed and celebrated with a bottle of local white wine until it was time for dinner and we walked slowly down the slope to the garden. The restaurant lay alongside the big pond under the cypress trees shading the tables from the blazing Midi sun. After the first few failures the owner of the restaurant came to recognize us and by now he greeted us warmly and told us with a smile that the next time would not be a failure. We knew, of course, that he did not mean it, and he knew we hoped the failures would continue. If we succeeded he would lose customers and we would be forced to find another challenge at which we could fail and celebrate with the dry local white wine. Finding another restaurant as good as this one would be difficult and we had enough difficulties already.

(1983)

227

A Short Conversation at Midday

THE HANDSOME YOUNG COUPLE sat on the café terrace facing the Place de la Republique and the old chateau that housed a museum devoted to a painter of abstract designs they had not heard of before. The day was hot and the sun hurt their eyes hidden behind large dark glasses. They had argued during the morning and were drinking pastis before lunch.

"Isn't this the loveliest day," she said with a smile. She had already forgotten the argument as she usually did soon after it was finished.

The young man nodded and drank the pastis so he would not have to answer.

"Don't you think this is what makes it all worthwhile," she said. "Lovely sunny days like this. Isn't it, baby?"

"Je ne crois pas," the young man said.

"No," she said, "that isn't quite right."

"What isn't quite right?" He immediately regretted asking the question.

"You left out the pronoun, silly. It. You left out the it."

"No," he said, "I didn't. Je ne crois pas."

And he looked away down the dusty road leading out of the village. Behind the dark glasses he squinted and whispered,

"Je ne crois pas."

(1986)

Romance on the Border

THE POET DID NOT WANT TO LEAVE THE BAR and they were having trouble convincing him. He did not make much loud noise and did not appear to be very drunk, but he was being stubborn about leaving. "I don't see why we have to go. It's not even midnight yet."

"They want to close up and go home. The festival starts early tomorrow. They want to get good seats in church," the woman who was with him explained. "So let's go. We can still catch the last bus across the border."

"We must close, señor, por favor," the bartender added hopefully.

The poet shook his head rapidly back and forth. "You don't understand. Vous ne comprend pas. I don't want to leave. I can't leave."

"Darling," she began, "be reasonable ..."

The poet began to shout. "Reason has nothing to do with it. Luck and talent, that's the stuff." He drank directly from the bottle on the table, spilling some of the wine on his yellow pullover. "I can't go back to France," he said sadly. "I can't leave this place."

The woman, at a loss for what to do, looked at the bartender who had seen it all too often before. He shrugged his shoulders slightly, looked at the almost empty wine bottle, and said, "Cinco minutos, no more."

The poet drank from the bottle again and reached for the last of his Spanish cigarettes. His gestures were determined and steady.

"Please," the woman began again.

"You don't understand," he said, speaking in a flat fast voice. "They won't take me alive. You see, I can't go back. Not for a long time. Perhaps never." He watched the dark blue Mediterranean water below them.

"I don't understand," she said beginning to consider leaving him there so she could catch the last bus over the border.

"Those poems I wrote this afternoon," he said with great seriousness. "They make Valéry no longer necessary. Maybe even Eluard. So you see, I can't leave here. I can't go back to France. They'll be waiting for me. What I've done is unforgivable."

(1985)

An Early Morning Wash

THE YOUNG GIRL dropped the last of her clothing on the narrow strip of pebbles between the water and the edge of the forest and walked cautiously into the lake. The Midi sun had burned away the early morning chill, but she shivered slightly and her nipples hardened. The night had not cooled the water in the lake and she eased gratefully into its silky comfort. Bending at the hips she splashed water on her skin and began to wash with a small piece of lavender soap. Her movements were languid and naturally sensual. The sun over the lake in the cypress and plane tree forest was just beginning to nip at her skin with its rays. She was happy that the family had decided not to go to the Côte d'Azur that summer ... it was much nicer and quieter here. As she stretched her browned body with the pleasure of the morning she did not see the creature with inflamed eyes creep out of the forest across the pebbles toward the water.

(Tavel, 1983)

Autumn Mornings in the Village

THE NOVEMBER MISTRAL blew very hard and cold, but the old women in the village walked about in the early morning hours with little more than sweaters and tradition to protect them. The pale sun offered a small touch of warmth if you stayed out of the wind. The women stopped between the boulangerie and the alimentation to exchange information and complaints, ignoring the cold and the wind, then moved on with purposeful but unhurried steps, holding their wicker baskets tightly. When we went out to buy fresh bread in the mornings when the mistral blew that autumn, we put on sweaters and heavy coats and wrapped scarves around our throats. The women did not laugh at us in our presence and we caught colds anyway.

(Tavel, 1982)

Against the Wall

THE YOUNG GYPSIES and the unemployeds huddled against each other and the wall for warmth in the dark, cold air. The mistral had begun to blow harshly through the streets of the ancient city of the popes. The yellow ramparts around the city had corroded into dull speckled gray as the 20th century continued its attack on the past. The unemployeds sat against the wall on the sufferance of the gypsies whose brief smiles admitted a contemptuous sympathy for them. A small illegal fire struggled against the wind and darkness and gave up no real warmth, but perhaps some comfort in its diminishing flames.

Each winter it was the same: almost no tourists, which meant less food and cold nights. The gypsies were preparing to return to their families for the waiting time until the spring and the tourists returned, the one as inevitable as the other. For the unemployeds, both foreign and domestic, it was different: most of them had no families to return to or that would accept them. For them, hunkered in their gray clothes against the mistral's bone-chill, spring was not so inevitable and they could not afford to wait for the tourists to return. Many would not see the one or the other next year, but there were always new unemployeds to take the places of the missing.

(Tavel, 1983)

High Summer in Provence

The heat bleeds away energy
Flies' bodies clog the typewriter
And the dog has ceased barking.

We batten down shutters against
The dry unexpected gusts that
Burn the bodies' fragile hairs
While flesh resists the heat with sweat
And brains slowly simmer in pots of bone.

When insects interrupt our reading
We become expert with fly swatters
In air too hot for music and we
Search the dull crushed sky in vain
For traces of the fabled Midi sunlight.

In a lemming rush for ease, progress,
We've bleached the sky with smoke and
        ashes
And live in memory of a sun-flooded south
We came too late to learn or penetrate.
Too much alive to the past, we

Encumber ourselves with nostalgia.
Dependent on churlishly accepted machines
We loudly yearn to adore the clean
        brilliance

Of this still magnetic landscape as we
Steer the car through the greenbrown
    garrigue

Thinking too much, complaining too much
While the cypress and olive trees rush by us.

(Nîmes, July 1983)

The Fishermen and the Poets

The fishermen and the poets have
Broken their lines so often
Both return in the evening with empty nets and
heads.

They sat too long alone
Waiting for something to bite
Both return in the evening with empty hands and
bellies.

Trying too hard with form
They never found the substance
Both return in the evening with empty eyes and
pockets.

Now the fishermen bring excuses or sneak off to
the market
The poets bring abandoned words tossed on pieces
of paper
Both return in the evening with empty hands and
heads.

(Tavel, 18.X.1983)

The New Monument: A Greek Village Fable

(For Alexina and David Ashcroft)

THE UNANNOUNCED and unintended construction of the new monument began on a typically bright sunny summer day, one of those for which the island of Corfu was famous in the tourist industry. The vendors in the narrow lanes of Corfu Town put out their chintzy wares early to accommodate the tourists disgorged by the massive cruise ships that dwarfed everything else in the new harbor and flocks of charter flights choking the airport. While the bulk of the tourists infested the town and the resorts along the coastline, the package tours for some included brief visits to quaint inland settlements. Here the villagers cranked up their artificial smiles and chopped English phrases for the omnibus loads of raucous bellowing red faces tumbling through the pneumatic doors onto the dusty narrow streets constructed before combustion engine vehicles had been invented.

It was, in fact, on the main street of one of these medieval villages, Perithia, which lies in the well of a small valley high in the island's northern mountains, that the new monument would stand for what the villagers that year would consider to be an eternity. And who is to say that, in the end, they were wrong?

What their starting point was, we do not know, and the records of the island's archives in the Old Fortress give no indication; we can assume, however, they were the high-rise resorts along the seashore. Regardless of their local origin, the two huge omnibuses, filled with what the town wags called in English "tourons," combining tourist and moron (no doubt unfairly since the island's economy required the presence of these creatures to survive), crawled slowly around the hairpin turns of the paved roads up the opposite sides of the mountain range like slow moving beetles hugging the surface to keep from flying off into the air, which was being unmercifully bludgeoned by their snarling engines.

Did the passengers enjoy the deep wide panoramas of the blue Ionian Sea? Could they smile at the vistas of dipping pine-covered valleys dotted by the occasional group of cypress trees jutting darkly out of the beige-green landscape? In their sealed air-cooled vehicles, equipped with television sets and on-board toilets, they certainly could not smell the scents of pine and sage that drifted over the roads down toward the sea. What they could do, and did with child-like gusto, is ignore the frustrated guide's attempts at humor and her informative lecture on the history of the flora and fauna they passed, preferring to gulp beer and chomp on onion and garlic flavored potato crisps, sweating (despite the air-cooled interior) and laughing at their own jokes and witticisms, red in face and neck, anxious that they receive every euro's value from this package holiday.

Dressed in the standard uniform of their trade: black trousers and blue shirts with the sleeves rolled up to the elbows, the bus drivers casually but with great care guided their metal monsters through hamlets and villages built several hundred years or more earlier, only occasionally knocking off pieces of masonry from the houses and stores whose façades stood far enough away from the streetbeds to allow easy passage for horse-drawn vehicles. The inhabitants of these giant tubes of glass and steel oohed and aahed as they passed close enough to the houses to reach out and shake hands with the owners if they had been able to open the bus windows and if the villagers had not shut their windows and shutters precisely to avoid seeing the shining heavy-jowled faces dotted with small squinting eyes leering into their living rooms.

At exactly 14 hours and 17 minutes on the 24-hour clock, the two buses entered Perithia's winding main street from opposite ends of the village, each followed by several automobiles whose drivers showed distinct signs of increasing impatience at the lumbering behavior of the behemoths. Halfway through the village the street narrows slightly, due to the construction of two three-story buildings on each side of the passageway, the result of two local families' competitive spirits and the use of cheap building materials several generations earlier. (The records of this competition are readily available in the archives, for those interested in Perithia's history.)

One and two-thirds minutes later the two buses stopped at the narrow section of the twisting road, facing each other like aging pre-historic beasts, neither wanting to retreat from the battle.

In fact, however, both drivers would have been happy to reverse their gearshifts and back up to allow the other to pass. They climbed out of their vehicles and joined the frustrated automobile drivers and several opinionated villagers, all of whom discussed the matter simultaneously and loudly in a manner which frightened the passengers, who viewed with alarm the violent gestures that accompanied the discussion. The tourists, not comprehending the nature of discussion natural to the Greek temperament, feared the disputants would soon come to blows.

Thirty-two minutes later the automobiles began to move backward out of the village until they reached runoffs where they could drive sufficiently off the road to allow one of the buses to back down to a space big enough to allow the other bus to pass by.

The problem, it soon became apparent, was that while the buses could drive forward through the village, the haphazard design of the roadway and the buildings precluded either one from moving out of the village in reverse gear. The two drivers and guides calmly climbed once again out of their vehicles, carefully closing the doors behind them to ensure the comfort of their increasingly restless charges. Once again the villagers, holding small cups of Greek coffee in their gnarled fingers, and the now exasperated expostulating automobile drivers joined the discussion on possible resolutions of this new problem.

The heated debate so absorbed the attention of both the discussants and the passengers that they did not at first notice the sudden darkening of the sky and the radical drop in the temperature. They did, however, notice the loud crack of thunder and the skittering flash of lightning that accompanied the traditional torrential downpour of the island's rain season. Indeed, as some of the villagers later said they remembered, the ear-splitting wrack of thunder and the jagged prongs of two massive lightning bolts that exploded on the buses threw the debaters away from the vehicles to the ground, thus saving their lives. The passengers on the buses did not enjoy the same fortune and all of them died instantly on those awkward positions humans, even tourons, assume if not strapped down when electrocuted.

At the same time, all the tires on the buses burst into shreds of evil smelling rubber, choking the air along with the acrid smoke and seared metal, leaving the omnibuses and all their modern conveniences sitting crouched on their broken axels and bent tire rims like two great brontosaurus about to spring at each other. This threat, clearly, they were no longer capable of transforming into action.

Indeed, after all the drivers and the villagers recovered what remained of their wits and called the police, several hospitals and the local fire department, they stood staring astounded at the remnants of the buses, which contained the dead tourists and smoldering cloth seats, the smell of which would have knocked them down had the glass shattered under the impact of the lightning, a phenomenon that had not, in fact, occurred, a situation no one was able to explain then or later. The observers knew not what action they should or could undertake. As a result, they undertook none and waited for some Authority to arrive to assume Responsibility.

For three days various Authorities came to examine the site and then left in their official vehicles to hold Meetings at Headquarters about what Should Be Done. Members of the fire department attempted to open the doors of the buses to remove the bodies, but the lightning had fused each vehicle into one unit of metal and glass that resisted all such efforts. It must also be admitted that the members of the fire department, being sensitive souls with sensitive Greek olfactory nerves, did not pursue the task of opening the curious tombs with very much enthusiasm. Finally they, too, left to report the matter to Higher Authority.

By the end of the fourth day, the villagers, unable to traverse the main street, began to use the footpath behind the row of buildings on the upper slope of the hillside parallel to the former but now impassable thoroughfare. After a while, when none of the Authorities could agree on which of them possessed the Responsibility for dealing with the unusual matter, the footpath became a narrow road and drivers began to use it in and out of the village on a regular basis.

The villagers began to transform what once had been the backs of the houses and stores on the main street into fronts, they planted gardens, added porches and the few shops remaining switched their counter and storage spaces to accommodate the new circumstances.

After the Engineering Authority from Athens declared the buses to be as hermetically sealed as pharaohs' graves, and after the Medical Authority, also from Athens, declared that the tourists' bodies would mummify without endangering the health of the local population, and after the deceased family members in the north of the continent declared themselves satisfied with death certificates in lieu of corpses (assisted by the Greek national government's transfer of certain funds into their bank accounts), after all this, which of course took a considerable amount of time, the villagers gradually became accustomed to the presence of the two behemoths, which gradually rusted and seemed to sink deeper into the earth as grass and other flora grew up around these hulks and their strange cargos.

Two generations after The Event, local officials held a ceremony to officially commemorate it, but no one could think of what exactly should be ceremonialized. They knew something should be memorialized because the Remnants had been there for so long, had indeed become something of a local attraction for the tourists who slowly returned to the village, and had become such a large presence in the region that they had to mean *something*.

After much debate they finally agreed upon the wording of a commemorative plaque that was so vague it could have meant anything, or nothing. On the appointed day, dressed in their uniform duty suits and hats, the officials unveiled the plaque and attached it to a tree that had grown between the two squatting relics. The village symphony consisting of three trumpets, a glockenspiel and a clarinet played the theme song from a popular American science fiction movie about wars in the future, which some may have considered inappropriate, but since this was the only music they had recently practiced it was the only piece all the amateur musicians knew well enough to play together. The officials made the requisite speeches, mercifully short because they did not really know what to say. The symphony reprised the movie score and everyone went home feeling they had Done Their Duty.

Three hundred and nine years later, a small group of archeology professors and students from the Ionian University in Butrint and the Nicaraguan Archeological Institute in Athens came to the now deserted village in search of artifacts from The Past. What they discovered astounded them and they spent days debating the meaning of their discovery. They typed up their field reports on their portable manual typewriters and, other forms of communications having been forbidden by the parliament of the World Government Organization in Calcutta, they telegraphed their reports from the post office of one of the two remaining villages on the island to Headquarters noting that, all things considered, the circumstances forced them to the conclusion that they had stumbled upon the remnants of a civilization that had committed suicide.

(Corfu & Key West 2004)

A Mediterranean Dream in Paris

I EXPERIENCED A DREAM the other night, strong, choked with starkly outlined images, unforgettable. Of course, I remembered very little of it and now must feebly reconstruct it as best I can, because it was a dream every human has had since before the first anthropocinian raised his arm before his eyes in terror millions of years ago: a vision of one's last day as a sentient being. Is this important? That is, would anyone other than me receive anything, even a modicum of pleasure at the minimum, from reading this? Otherwise why would I be sitting here in this cramped Paris hotel room, alone on a Saturday night, before me an ever diminishing bottle of Tavel rosé and several small green bottles of Badoit mineral water, sweating profusely into my Ivan Karamazov collarless shirt, writing this down on a square-lined page of a Bloc bureau 80 feuilles format 210x320 quadrillé séyès papier sufin 80 g?

It is true that the clarity of my handwriting diminishes in proportion to the decrease in the bottle's content. Everyone understands this, and, one hopes, makes the necessary adjustments in their minds. I should not forget to note that I write this Rousseauian confession with a disposable

Pilot fountain pen – encre noir – which so perfectly symbolizes our current situation in the west: everything is made for us so cheaply in the east that one need not renew it: throw it away when depleted – no reason to refill.

So. Who appears in this dream? Will we all recognize them, those fortunates who will come to life and breathe the austere air, so pure and dead, of a dream? What is its structure? About its meaning we can debate later – or you can, since I will no longer be here to entertain you. After all, this is a dream about my last day alive – and we all deeply believe in the predictive power of dreams, do we not?

The terrace at the Colombe d'or in Saint-Paul-de-Vence, situated in the hills above Cannes on the Mediterranean shore: if you sit at the edge of the terrace you can see the long, narrow valley below the hill on which the village perches. It is a particularly satisfying sight – or was – because the implacable surges of human greed have not fouled the steep hills with bungalows for the rich and stupid, and you can, or could, still enjoy the untrammeled greens and beiges and browns of the southern Provençal landscape. On the terrace, at some unspecified, and from my point of view very much future time, did the dream play itself out.

Of course, it was a dream of a long, well-watered lunch in the autumn when the sun still warms the terrace at midday, but does not oppress the diners, and a mild breeze gently caresses the guests, especially the guest of honor, who does not sweat and who can breathe freely. There are very good reasons why Yves Montand, Simone Signoret, James Baldwin, and many other well-known people have chosen to live here, and even larger numbers of people, some of whom you would not necessarily invite to lunch, come here throughout the year to bask in the glories of the Mediterranean light. Lynn-Marie and I must be counted among them, but you would of course invite *us* to lunch. And these reasons do not necessarily include the quality of the kitchen's production, if one insists upon the most exquisite meal one has ever had: we have always eaten well and marvelously here, but one does not expect two-star Michelin quality (the third star has naught to do with the food, but tells you something about the ambience of the experience you might have if you visit). Perhaps the very lack of expectation contributes to the massive sense of pleasure that washes over one as one eats there on that terrace in the sun.

All of my friends came to my final luncheon event: Alberto Giacometti tried his best to infest the air with the smoke from his unfiltered Pall Mall cigarettes, but realized the impossibility of his task, though he did not give up. He made a tiny pressed-bread sculpture of Lynn-Marie out of half a baguette's insides.

Yves leaned over and asked me to make some time later for a game of boules on the square outside the restaurant's walls. He insisted that we change into white clothes before we joined him: apparently his contract with the village called for a white costume readily identifiable by the press and tourists. We agreed because just that morning my white burial suit had been delivered from the terminal Panamanian tailor in Nice who specializes in such things. My friend Matisse had told me about this fellow and highly recommended his work. He had dressed the old painter for years before he finally bid the world adieu. What better recommendation could one have? Henri had to leave before the lunch was over, to pay a call on our mutual acquaintance, Pierre Bonnard, who was recovering from major surgery a few kilometers away in Les Cannettes, but we were able to exchange a few affectionate words and I slipped him some naughty postcards for old Pierre. Then his nurse wheeled him through the crenellated gate to the small limousine parked outside. The chauffeur had to be awakened from his dream of being fellated by Senta Berger in a field of lavender. The great smile of bliss that lit that young thug's face inspired the painter to sketch another odalisque sucking a strawberry lollypop lying on a bed of fennel leaves on the Moroccan seashore.

A few tables from ours the Murphy's and their hopelessly gauche friends sat laughing and drinking white wine laced with fresh lime juice over ice cubes that the vacuous juice prevented from sparkling in the flashing yellow sunshine. Their children were perfectly behaved and clearly enjoyed the antics of their elders, even if they did not care for the succulent calamari or the fabulously grilled rougets. They did drink their kirs with some gusto, however, and did not seem the worse for that wear.

Anita Berber flitted about in a series of veils of changing colors and nothing else. When she came to brush her lips against my cheek I caught the distinct odors of opium and Coca-Cola. She did not require any music to underscore her dance. At one point she flitted to the Mann family's long table and threw herself on to Tommy's lap, whispering in to his hairy ear certain things about Joseph and his coat of many colors; Katja was not pleased, but her husband and father of their six uproarious children smiled in warm confusion, wondering how he would describe the scene in his diary later that evening.

Brigitte stopped by briefly on her way up from Saint Tropez to the ancient Roman city of Orange to join the battle against the dark foreign intrusions who were despoiling French national honor. She didn't look a day older than 25 and some at the tables repeated the rumor that it was the desperate energy she threw into the battle to save all the wild dogs on the Côte d'Azur that kept her magnetic physical presence so blatantly attractive. Another rumor had it that she was writing her memoirs with the same ghost writer who penned le Pen's speeches, and that the contents would preclude publication in Islamic countries. One wag murmured that this did not matter because no one in those regions had ever heard of her. When she and her pack of snarling canines swept through the gate to their SUV, a distinct sigh of relief wafted across the terrace. Anita sneered and wagged her small tail. The Murphy kids laughed out loud. Yves shrugged his expressive shoulders and turned to Simone murmuring, "Quien sabe?"

I was particularly pleased to see Jimmy Baldwin and waved him and his friend over to our table so they could pay their last respects. I asked him to stop by the hotel for a drink in the crepuscule of the early evening so we could talk about some streets in New York City's Greenwich Village where we had both lived for a while, though at separate epochs. He murmured darkly that he loved the warmth and the sun, and was at peace with himself, working on a novel and resisting without much success the demands of his friends in America that he travel around that place, speaking about integrating the Negroes into the mainstream. Consequently, our meeting would have to wait for some time when he had the time, and anyway, he said, thinking about the good old days in the Village upset his equipoise. I refrained from reminding him that my own equipoise was not very much longer for this world and that, under the circumstances, the meeting would in all probability therefore never take place. We kissed and he returned to his table with his friend to eat his vegetarian meal and drink a bottle of Sancerre all by himself. His friend, whose name was actually Adamo, whom he'd met in a small café in Istanbul, drank mineral water to maintain his own equipoise.

At this point, short and burly Lawrence Durrell, knitted bright Greek blue woolen scarf trailing stiffly behind him, shot on to the terrace, as if propelled by some ancient Hellenic blood-feud legend, careened around the seated and standing participants waving a half full bottle of cold Tavel rosé about him with great abandon, singing a Zen Buddha yoga melody filled with narky quartertones and stumbled into Jimmy's table, recognized him after a bleery second, and, laughing at great volume crushed, the slender figure in a bear hug. "Saviour!" he yelled, or was it "Sancerre!"? And plopped himself down at the table, took a giant swig of the rosé and began to vigorously discuss the difference between the Negro and Caucasian approaches to the practice of standing on one's head in the lotus position in the shower before six in the morning. Later he came over to our table and attempted to convince us that the Macabru's theory of death being the ultimate expression of life was the only sane way to face either one.

Fortunately, he was interrupted by the rolly-polly poet, Jacques Prévert, who, despite his name, was an exemplar of the city-dweller slumming in the sun-washed countryside, a half-lighted Gauloise permanently pasted in the corner of his mouth, who now staggered to the top of his table covered with plates full of butt ends and ashes and bottles of that quality red wine the British refer to as plonk, and demanded attention. Announcing he was about to recite a new poem, written specifically for this august occasion, he wasted no time in doing so, perhaps fearing that any pause might lead to his removal by the exasperated hovering waiters and the ever-ready large figure of Georges Braque, who had practiced bouncing obstreperous friends and acquaintances from the scenes of their perversions since the Great War. After all, once a poet began to recite, what Frenchman could interrupt a work of art being proclaimed? Speaking rapidly, as all Frenchmen do, Prévert grandly informed us that he had titled the ode, "The Rats Leave the Three-Skeleton Key Lighthouse." No one on the terrace of the Columbe d'or that day, or any other day for that matter, comprehended the appropriateness of this particular poem for the occasion, but the applause at the end washed over him like a dose of chloroform and I recognized the sly glint of conspiracy in his eye before he fell asleep, his head resting comfortably on the rim of his red wine glass, into which his Gauloise had precipitously fallen.

Braque was his usual reticent self, secretly glad that his erstwhile co-inventor of Cubism decided not to leave his castle an hour's drive away, though he did send an autographed caricature of himself as an old crone, delivered by his chauffeur who is in reality one of his ne'er-do-well sons given employment at a discounted salary. After telling me all about his latest illness, which he insisted had totally incapacitated him for months, Braque strode carefully on old boxer's feet through the office-bar to the swimming pool decorated with his own bird and, quickly stripping off his clothes, leaped into the over-chlorinated water and swam laps for the following 58 minutes, singing an old Charles Trenet song at the top of his voice. The owner shrugged his narrow shoulders and mumbled something to the effect that artists are granted more leeway in their behaviors than other human folk.

The headwaiter had just placed before us the first course of giant crawfish accompanied by an explosively garlicked aïoli when a sudden rustling of shifting feet and chairs announced the arrival of additional friends at the gate to the terrace. A bearded bald sun-browned head cautiously looked around the corner of the gate as if to determine whether or not it was safe to enter and, seeing the raucous rowdies populating the tables on the terrace, jerked back out of sight. "Paulie!" I bellowed, "get back in here and sit down!" One normally doesn't bellow at a man as shy and sensitive as the scion of the Cézanne family, but this was not a normal day by any means. And the old fellow did in fact enter the terrace around the massive bronze thumb of our great friend César, the junk man sculptor, pushing a bright pink wheelchair occupied by a small, sharply bearded, retiring figure with paint brushes strapped to his arthritic hands which he waved at everyone with joyous abandon.

At a corner table under the lilac tree a perfectly coiffed Chagall scowled at his plate of olives coated with thyme and oil from the lamps of China. Perhaps the construction of the museum to house his Biblical murals was not going quite on schedule, or perhaps it was the Russian Jewish soul that cringed at the idea of being happy at such an occasion. I decided to speak with him of other things, to take his mind off whatever troubled him. At the next table, deep in conversation that absorbed all their energies, Jean-Paul Belmondo, Macha Meril and Michel Simon discussed the limitations on roles for actors as they aged into antiquity. What, after all, can one do when one can no longer swing from a rope down from the first balcony onto the stage? The discussion, I knew, would last for years, like the Jerusalem poker game. In fact, it had no ending at all.

What really broke the place up was the stumbling entry of Jacques Clouseau, some time inspector of the Parisian police, sagely looking about him inspecting the guests with that sharp eye, demanding an answer to that ancient Socratic question, "Does youah dawgy bahyt?" Two uniformed carabinieri finally escorted him to the waiting squad car and ougah-ougahed him to the railroad station, whence he traveled at TGV speed to his next case in Arcachon where he intended to meet his former colleague, Monsieur Pampelmousse and his canine sidekick, Pommes Frites, to solve the mystery of the sickly oyster.

A sudden roar from the swimming pool astonished everyone by its volume and intensity; indeed it seemed hardly human such was its agonized bawl that shot out across the terrace and out over the valley, disturbing Canetti's goats as they scampered erratically up and down the slopes. This mystery soon resolved itself: the Murphy children had slipped one of the chef's live lobsters into the pool and this seaborne creature had attached one of its pinchers to the lap-swimming Braque's left testicle with some intensity, thus motivating what was, essentially, his cri de coeur for assistance. This was forthcoming in the form of two sous-chefs with hammers and tongs, and before long the agonized painter found himself lying naked on the edge of the pool freed of his encumbrance and very red in the face and scrotum.

In order to fill the sound vacuum left by the cessation of Braque's bellowing, a small group of men, fists full of glasses brimming with pastis and tiny French ice cubes, gathered near the entrance to the bar. Yves Montand the pétanque player; Charles Aznavour the diminutive Armenian puffing a Broyard; long-haired smiling Jean Ferrat, mustaches flairing, looking very much like a cavalier in drag; Georges Brassens with the bristling mustache and bad reputation, his pipe at the ready; Leo Ferré on the verge of hysteria pulling his long stringy hair; Jacques le Belge grinning his ape grin with a string of purple orchids around his neck; the transplanted American Eddie Constantine, a book of Eluard's poems sticking out of his trench coat pocket, keys to the white Mustang in his hand; and the leather-jacketed pseudonymous Johnny Hallyday, vigorously battering his unplugged guitar; all broke into a rowdy but melodic cabaret number written especially for the occasion by Lennie Ravel, the apprentice busboy recently hired by the management. Their rhythmic movements were choreographed with the precision of the Rockettes or an amateur (the best kind) street corner doowop group bopping their fingers and snapping their toes in unison – the perfect accompaniment to the song whose title, we later discovered, was "Shuffling Off This Mortal Coil in Technicolor."

Several choruses do not translate well from the original Hindi text Lennie Ravel found one night in the basement of the Majarubi's castle near the Sanjack of Novi Basar's southern border. However, Prévert later gave me a wine-soaked slip of paper with his rendering of two of them.

> *O crooked man*
> *Bent to the wind*
> *Zip up your doodah*
> *Chop up your dinde*
> > *Doo-oo-oo-oo-ahh*

> *The pale moon sets me off*
> *Just like Howdee Doodah*
> *Clamor for the revelation*
> *What is that you do dah?*
> > *Doo-oo-oo-oo-waaahhh!*

At the end of the afternoon, as the crepuscule crept over yon russet-clad hill, and the sunlight began to turn blue and ochre, the ever beautiful and dapper Hans Albers slipped through the groaning but hardly bored crowd and, accompanied by my brother Dean on the Caribbean pans, began to sing in that world-famous whisky tenor.

Goodbye, Johnny,
Goodbye, Johnny,
Schön war's mit uns zwei,
aber leider, aber leider,
kann's nicht immer so sein.
Goodbye, Johnny,
Goodbye, Johnny,
Macht's mir nicht so schwer.
Ich muß weiter, immer weiter,
meinen Glück hinterher.
Bricht mir heut' das Herz in zwei,
In hundert Jahren, Johnny,
Ist doch alles vorbei -
Johnny!

Which means something along the lines of: "We had a great time together/ but it's too bad/ it's too bad/it can't always be so/Goodbye Johnny/goodbye Johnny/Don't make it so hard for me/I must go on/ever onward/chasing my fortune/Today you break my heart in two/in a hundred years, Johnny/it'll all be over/Johnny!" Rather appropriate for the occasion we all agreed, though my name has to my knowledge never been John.

Here the dream must have ended or perhaps it went on just a bit longer to witness the departure of all those friends and relatives into the deepening Mediterranean night where no mosquitoes sting, as quickly and as silently as they appeared, leaving me alone on the pale moon lit terrace to face that final question, "Does *mah* dawgy bahyt?"

(Paris, 4.XI.1999)

The Olive Tree and the Mistral

(For Susan Stiers MacNiven, in memoriam)

TO THE LEFT BELOW THE TERRACE outside the kitchen, an olive tree bends before the mistral. The confrontation occurs throughout the year whenever the wind blows. There is no victor, no defeated, and the struggle will continue until the tree dies. The other olive and cypress trees near this particular one do not bear so much of the wind's savagery. I do not know the reason for this, nor can anyone in the village with whom I've talked explain the matter. I've come to think this is a special olive tree.

When the mistral blows it is unrelenting in its force and duration. The people of Provence place large stones on the tiled roofs of their houses and barns, although modern technology has devised a glue to hold the tiles down, and one sees forms of plastic or polyurethane panels being bolted on to the frames of some wine warehouses. Since it lasts for three or six or nine days (time always mystically divisible by three) on each occasion, this construction is viewed in the Midi as progress.

There is a crevice somewhere in the house through which the wind seethes with a peculiar intermittent keening, as if lamenting the disappearance of winter. When this singing rattle

263

combines with the long whoosh of the surging air, it can madden the brain and bruise the emotions. In Munich during a certain season when the dry sterile wind called the Föhn blows out of the Alpine valleys, judges have been known to take it into consideration as an extenuating circumstance when sentencing transgressors of the law. The Provençaux do not see the mistral as an accessory before the fact in cases of murder and adultery, but they do understand a certain withdrawal from the world, in season, as when one neighbor passes another in the street without a word of greeting. "Ah, c'est seulement le mistral."

During the late fall and winter, the mistral brings with it a radical drop in temperature. The streets empty and one's fuel bill rises to astronomical levels: houses here are built for the long hot summer months, not to withstand the sharp winter blasts, and the northern art of insulation is practically unknown here. In the spring, when the mistral rips down the Rhône Valley to the sea, the temperature drop is not so precipitous and if one faces the south in a warm sweater one can sit on the terrace without shivering.

I have often been struck by an unusual aspect of this southern wind in winter: the sun continues to shine with its unique luminosity in a clear blue-gray sky during the height of the storm. Some who live here will tell you the mistral washes the sky, satisfied that the sun shines so brightly during the cold winter months. If the mistral is the price to be paid for this, ça va! That is why in Provence no windows are built facing north: the people of the Midi do not care much for those in the north in any case - they speak strangely and, like lunatics, demand everything be done immediately.

"When will it end?" I cried one day at the garage. The mechanic smiled briefly and made that traditional French gesture of bowing to the inevitable, a shrug of the shoulders. "Il fait beau, monsieur, le soleil est chaud. Alors!" And so it is.

But a constant layer of sandy yellow dust covers everything; and the constant rustling of the rose bushes and pine trees in Madame Mourre's garden, the continual pressure against one's body while walking, the high-pitched rattling in that undiscovered crevice, the sight of that olive tree enduring - these things can lead the faint of heart and fragile of emotion to question their own perspectives, to doubt their very reason. The mistral is nothing if not fundamental.

In Provence they have learned to live with this climatic oddity's grating presence, to limit the damage it does to their property and their souls. Occasionally, of course, a piece of tile roof, red-orange in the sun, flies through the air to shatter on the ground or on the hood of an unlucky automobile; only rarely does the missile actually kill anyone.

The mistral also plays havoc with certain results of technological progress. It is not unusual to be driving through a deserted garrigue in the Gard and have the eye assaulted by the sight of bright blue plastic bags corrupting the barren landscape with progress the mistral refuses to recognize. All over the region, wind-shredded pieces of this garbage bag blight the harsh beauty of the natural landscape, flapping in the shrubbery of the brown-green fields and hills, reinforcing the widely-held notion that the French are not particularly concerned with cleanliness. The Provençaux, of course, blame it on the foreign tourists (which include all of the French north of Valence) and the Gypsies. The mistral shows no mercy; only humans are capable of that gesture.

The snapping mistral certainly shows none to my olive tree just below the terrace. The tree and the mistral deal with each other in blind obedience to laws which we can describe, but for which we have no satisfactory explanation. I write "my" olive tree, although it belongs to Madame Mourre and we are but visitors to the village. However, to a large degree it *is* my olive tree, for I have appropriated it in my mind. On loan, perhaps, but for the moment I consider it mine. In the same way, the feeling of belonging, being part of the landscape, however briefly, is strong within me. (The fact that my awkward, hesitant attempts at the language must appear rather drôle to my neighbors is less relevant than one might think. We do communicate whatever is necessary, even hold short conversations, usually about the weather, about the mistral. In any case, I am able to buy groceries and wine, and I have learned to understand some of the language, even in its provençal accents, if not to speak it. I have become very practiced at listening intently.)

The olive tree has become both an ideal to live up to and a companion that gives comfort in hours of doubt, those unsettling moments of despair which cannot be truly explained to others, no matter how much one loves them. The thin-branched olive tree does not smoke too many cigarettes, nor drink too much wine, nor weep secretly in frustration. It withstands the savage battering of the mistral, the relentless twisting and pummeling of its trunk and branches, its leaves maintain their grip under the pounding pressure. At times bent in half by the atavistic, seemingly vengeful wind, it survives, it remains when the storm moves south toward the Mediterranean. It *resists* the strength of the mistral and the summer sun with its own strength and resilience. My olive tree not only survives these irregular attacks: each year it produces its quota of olives and it will continue to do so until it exhausts itself and is replaced in another millennium. It produces its fruit, its raison d'être.

Often, standing on the terrace, eyes narrowed against the wind, I watch the roaring mistral whip its branches back and forth, and I experience an exultation, a rush of soaring emotion not easily described but burstingly felt, that must approximate the emotion of a god: I can create the universe! Or at least *some* universe. Whether or not I rush to the desk and take up my pen is of no matter at such moments. I am restored in faith and balance; I can face time with courage if not optimism. I will not only overcome my weaknesses, I will triumph in my art. At the very least I will finish my book and it will be good. As the olive tree survives the mistral's onslaught, I will survive the agony of my doubts and the indifference of society. As the tree produces olives at the end of the procreative cycle, I will produce what I must.

This slender green tree so battered by the brutal mistral has become for me what O. Henry's last leaf was for the tubercular young girl in that shabby boarding house in the early urban nightmare. But my olive tree is not painted on an alley wall in a slagheap of human dreams. My olive tree is as real as the mistral that tortures its boughs with a vicious intensity, but cannot destroy it.

(Tavel, 1982)

268

Index

Printed in the United States
26354LVS00001B/149